LIVING WITH
Lace

LIVING WITH

Lace

BO NILES

PRINCIPAL PHOTOGRAPHY BY GEORGE ROSS

DESIGN BY JULIO VEGA

STEWART, TABORI & CHANG
NEW YORK

Text copyright © 1990 Bo Niles
Photographs copyright © 1990 George Ross
Due to limitations of space, photo credits appear on page
170 and constitute an extension of this page.

Published in 1990 by
Stewart, Tabori & Chang, Inc.
575 Broadway, New York, New York 10012

Library of Congress Cataloging-in-Publication Data

Niles, Bo.
Living with lace/Bo Niles; principal photography by George Ross.
p.   cm.
Includes bibliographical references.
ISBN 1-55670-156-X: $29.95
1. Textile fabrics in interior decoration.   2. Lace and lace
making.   I. Ross, George, 1959–   II. Title.
TX315.N55   1990
645′.046—dc20
90-34556
CIP

Distributed in the U.S. by Workman Publishing,
708 Broadway, New York, New York 10003
Distributed in Canada by Canadian Manda Group,
P.O. Box 920 Station U, Toronto, Ontario M8Z 5P9
Distributed in all other territories by
Little, Brown and Company, International Division,
34 Beacon Street, Boston, Massachusetts 02108

Printed in Japan

10   9   8   7   6   5   4   3   2   1

For Sally

CONTENTS

THE LURE OF LACE

How this fragile and beautiful fabric
came to captivate the European aristocracy,
and why its popularity endures

9

THE LOVE OF LACE

How laces, old or new, can enhance
every room in the house, from living room to bath,
and even the backyard or beach

25

THE LOOK OF LACE

How to care for and store lace,
where to find antique and new lace,
and selected readings to enjoy

151

DIRECTORY
163

CREDITS
170

ACKNOWLEDGMENTS
173

INDEX
174

THE LURE OF LACE

*L*ace. A whisper of a name for a whisper of a textile. The most gentle, fluid, and delicate of fabrics, lace enjoys a romantic reputation: think of the butterfly caress of a bridal veil or the winsome touch of lace at a collar or cuff; of a hint of lace sewn onto a handkerchief peeking out of a pocket or sleeve; or the alluring flirt of lace along the hem of a petticoat or negligee. Consider a lace-edged bureau scarf resting upon a rosewood dresser, or a crocheted doily under a teacup; lace curtains kissed by a zephyr at the window, or a cutwork bedcover tumbled back among the sheets of a four-poster bed, itself canopied with lace.

working conditions and who were prohibited by class distinction—and by law—from wearing their own creations. Ironically, many laces were delivered to their patrons to be used just once, then tossed aside or packed away; if fashion had changed, the laces might be rejected altogether. When revered, lace was more precious than currency, more valuable than gemstones. When reviled, it was burned or torn into rags.

Legends abound regarding the true origins of lace. Venice and Antwerp both lay claim to the earliest European textiles identified as laces, which predated the Renaissance. Other coastal areas—in England, Denmark, and the French provinces of Brittany and Normandy—also document textiles that evolved into lace; the British, for example, allude to pre-Elizabethan efforts in making lace using needles and bobbins made from fishbones. These earliest textiles all exhibit a common interlacing, much the same as that used in basketry; or a knotting and tying into a mesh, as in a net, trap, or snare. The word *lace* derives from "lacis," which means "snare," but can also mean the task of darning net. And these early lacemaking areas began generating laces as a cottage industry to supplement their occupational mainstay, fishing, during periods of inclement weather.

Because lace is so extraordinarily fine, it is associated with sentimental events that inspire tender recollections, thoughts, and fantasies: birth, christening, courtship, seduction, marriage. Lace is a textile that celebrates grace.

The history of lace, however, is a cruel story, fraught with conflict and controversy. At the height of its popularity, from the sixteenth through the eighteenth centuries, lace was the ultimate status symbol, and a major emblem by which aristocratic nobles could flaunt their wealth and curry favor with the reigning monarch. But these laces—all made by hand—were the product of months and even years of labor. They were designed and created by craftspeople (almost all of them women) who endured abject poverty and grim

Historians assume that primitive forms of lace—those predating the Renaissance—were worked on pieces of loose-woven cloth, usually linen, which were cut or pierced. The threads were then pulled together ("drawn") to create holes [*punto tirato*], or one or more threads were removed ("withdrawn") to achieve a similar effect [*punto tagliato*]. The holes were reinforced around their edges to prevent raveling.

Because they were defined by the right angles created by the warp and weft threads of a plain cloth or a net mesh, the punto tirato or tagliato patterns were geometric in design. To vary the pattern, the needleworker might fill in some of the holes, or partially fill them in, and thus create subordinate motifs to complement the overall design. The dictionary of lace written and compiled by British authority Pat Earnshaw defines lace as "a textile patterned with holes which are created by manipulating threads"; Webster's Dictionary calls lace "an openwork, usually figured fabric, made of thread or yarn and used for trimmings, household coverings, and entire garments."

In its earliest guise, lace was rendered in narrow bands—no wider than an inch or so—that could be applied as borders to the edges of a piece of cloth or as strips inset between pieces of cloth. The borders or insets served an important function, which was to reinforce the frayed edges of the existing cloth and thus prolong the life of a garment or household linen, much as darning or mending might. It soon became apparent, however, that such borders or insets could also embellish or decoratively enhance the piece of cloth. The first such embellishments seem to have been reserved for ecclesiastical cloths (of course, household linens and personal clothing, used daily, deteriorated long ago and have been lost to our scrutiny, so it is somewhat unfair to make this assumption).

As needleworkers attained a certain proficiency and became more innovative in technique, they found they could manipulate the

293. - Le Leveur de Dentelles

reinforcing or outlining thread, and the filling thread as well, without a mesh to guide the stitches. The thread itself, rather than any supporting backcloth, became both the armature and the instrument of design. The Italians named this liberated textile *punto in aria* or "stitches in air," and freethread designs, again with no fabric base, *reticella.*

The Germans and Italians, appreciating the increased complexity and subtlety of design possible

A French postcard from the 1890s depicts a quartet of lacemakers from Provence chatting amiably as they work.

11

within the reticella and punto in aria formats, began to publish pattern books, which spread the most popular designs to a general public. In her research, Pat Earnshaw tallies over 400 editions of 156 pattern books published during the sixteenth century alone. With the publication of these books, and consequent transmittal of design and technique, the manufacture of lace began to spread more and more rapidly throughout Europe —and the popularity of lace burgeoned. Lacemaking became a full-fledged industry, requiring technicians of superb skill to execute the ever-more-sophisticated designs required by a demanding and discerning clientele.

When a plainweave cloth or mesh had provided the armature for a design, its grid, as noted, dictated a geometric pattern, but once the threads were liberated from their whole-cloth background, the outline of the design and the design itself could be manipulated with greater flexibility and in various ways: in how the outline was laid down, in how it was reinforced, in how the spaces between the outlines could be filled, and in how the various open and filled areas, or individual motifs within the design, were connected. One Venetian publisher's pattern books, produced over a twenty-year period during the 1500s, visually document the evolution of design from the purely geometric to the sinuously curvilinear.

If the lacemaker relaxes the tension on the outlining thread, the thread begins to sag or curl. Rather than being pulled taut, as in a grid, the sagging thread could be reinforced or held firm just as it was placed, in a curve. Being able to move the threads freely and reinforce them afterward allowed for increased creativity; over time, the rigid geometries of mesh-defined designs gave way to liquid, lyrical shapes, such as curves and scrolls, and, later still, flowers, vines, and even realistically detailed humans, animals, birds, and architectural motifs.

Handmade laces were created by two different methods. One of these, needle lace, is described by Pat Earnshaw as "constructed of buttonhole stitches." A needle is used to manipulate the stitches according to a predetermined design. The buttonhole stitch, which comprises a loop with a half-caught knot, offers seemingly limitless maneuverability. A piece of needle lace can vary greatly in length and

breadth, and in delicacy and artistry, limited only by the dimensions of the pattern and the skill of the lacemaker. In studying specific examples of needle lace, textile historians have calculated over eighty variations upon the button-hole stitch.

Bobbin lace, by contrast, relies on the manipulation of multiple threads. Each thread is slung over and suspended from one pin in a row of pins piercing the top, or

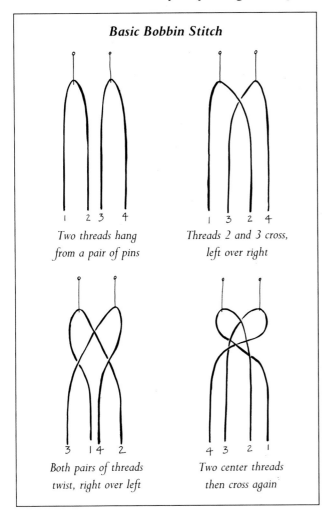

Basic Bobbin Stitch

1 2 3 4	1 3 2 4
Two threads hang from a pair of pins	*Threads 2 and 3 cross, left over right*
3 1 4 2	4 3 2 1
Both pairs of threads twist, right over left	*Two center threads then cross again*

"heading," of an outlined pattern, which the pins secure to a pillow. For this reason, bobbin lace has been called "pillow lace." The lacemaker rests the pillow across her lap or upon a frame. The threads are wrapped around bobbins; the bobbins weight the threads.

The lacemaker creates her design by maneuvering one pair of

bobbins, or "leaders," crossing them over or twisting them around each pair of threads—moving from pair to pair, starting from the right and working to the left, and back, according to the pattern, much as any weft thread is maneuvered through a warp on a loom today. The wider the piece of lace, and the finer the thread, the more bobbins were required. Working with six dozen bobbins to create a lace a few inches wide was a commonplace practice. In some cases, more than one lacemaker could work at a single pillow; one documented piece was worked on by four women, each lacemaker using fifteen dozen bobbins. Bobbin laces could be made as continuous pieces, with the "motif" or design element and "ground" or background as one, or as noncontinuous pieces with the motifs crafted separately and then joined to the ground to create the finished product.

Mrs. Bury Palliser, a self-taught connoisseur of lace who wrote a charming history on the subject over a century ago, believed from her observations, that bobbin laces grew more popular in Northern Europe while needle laces dominated in Southern Europe—although neither method was exclusive to its area.

For both types of lace, the linen thread woven of flax grown in what is now Belgium was preferred. This flax was strong, tensile, and durable, and could be spun into exceedingly fine thread. The thread was revered for its purity of texture and for its color—so pale as to appear almost pure white. Occasionally, lacy cloth was made of filaments of gold and silver, but the cost of metallic thread was usually prohibitive, and flax proved a suitable and more affordable substitute.

As the art of lacemaking became more sophisticated, laces became more intricate. Eventually, the task of creating a piece of lace suitable for fashionable attire became too complex for a single lacemaker to accomplish without consuming an inordinate amount of time; assembly-line techniques began to be applied, saving time —and time, then as now, was money. According to Mrs. Palliser: "It would take one lacemaker twelve hours a day twelve years to complete a piece of lace eighteen feet long—and that works out to one-third of an inch a week." At the Paris Exhibition of 1889, Mrs. Palliser admired a single piece of lace made in Alençon, a major lacemaking center in Normandy, that had required sixty-five thousand working days to complete! It became the exception rather than the rule for a piece to be commissioned as a single unit produced by one lacemaker.

Thousands of lacemakers were required to meet the incoming orders. As lace burgeoned in popularity, more and more of the female population in the major lacemaking centers—in France, Belgium, and Italy, above all—entered this profession. At its apogee, lacemaking employed over half a million women and girls throughout Europe, over 250,000 in France alone. By the mid-nineteenth century one-quarter of the entire female population of Belgium was involved in making lace.

Many lacemaking schools affiliated themselves with convents, thus taking advantage of a ready-made, self-contained work force. Families with many children (and too many mouths to feed) were grateful to the convents for recruiting their younger daughters. Little girls, often as young as five, were provided room and board in exchange for their training and were expected to serve an apprenticeship of a decade or more. The children learned one procedure at a time—from creating an outline to filling in a motif to preparing a background—progressing from one task to the next as they became proficient in the skill required for each. By their teens, the girls would be skilled enough to seek independent employment, or they could be put on retainer to the shop associated with the school. Upon graduation, many lacemakers chose or were assigned a specialty, and worked in that capacity for the remainder of their careers. Proficiency in a single process ensured precision, precision led to perfection, and perfection to speed.

In a needle lace school and shop, for example, a mistress-lacemaker, the head of the shop, would display her particular, and signature, selection of designs to the client. The designs and motifs, which often became identified with the particular shop and with the town where it was located, were jealously guarded. The mistress-lacemaker would then devise any alterations that the client might require, and would finally develop the pattern. The design would be outlined, or pricked out with pins, upon a strip of vellum. The pricking served as a guide for the lacemaker given the assignment of stitching the outline. The pricking would then be attached to a sleeve of cloth to hold it in place. As the lacemaker worked, she would catch the outlining strand at intervals along the vellum, sewing through both vellum and sleeve, to steady the strand and secure it for the lacemakers responsible for later procedures. To vary the outline and to add visual richness, she might "raise" or reinforce the strand so that it would stand out from the rest of the stitching.

Once the outline was completed, another lacemaker would fill in the spaces between the outlined strands to create the requisite design motifs. The motifs in turn would be connected to one another—by yet another lacemaker—by stitches that also formed the supporting ground. These stitches were called brides or bars. Sometimes lacemakers punctuated the brides with knots called picots.

𝒞onditions in both school and shop were grim. The lacemakers rose before dawn. Their workday typically commenced at 4 A.M., and they worked long into the night, by candlelight—totaling eighteen hours of labor.

Because linen thread and lace could—and would—soil easily during the time required to execute a piece, lacemakers were not allowed to work near a fire, even during the winter, as smoke would surely sully their work. In France, it is said, some lacemakers spent their winter hours working in sheds near the animals, to garner what precious little heat they could from the warmth and breath of the beasts.

For many adult lacemakers, their craft—despite the long work day—was supplemented by household chores. Little wonder many lacemakers died young of illnesses such as tuberculosis. And thousands of lacemakers became blind before the age of thirty.

Mrs. Palliser describes at length the work day at a lace school in England operating during her own lifetime. In this particular venue, children began their training at the ripe age of eight; their workday lasted twelve hours.

. . . Here the hours were from 6 A.M. in the summer and from 8 A.M. to 8 P.M. in the winter. Half an hour was allowed for breakfast and for tea, and one hour for dinner, so that there were ten hours for actual work. The girls had to stick ten pins a minute, or six hundred an hour, and if at the end of the day they were five pins behind, they had to work for another hour. . . . They could earn about sixpence a day. Pay-day was a great event; it came once a month. . . . On the evenings 18 girls worked by one tallow candle, value one penny; the "candle-stool" stood about as high as an ordinary table with four legs. In the middle of this was what was known as the "pole-board," with six holes in a circle and one in the centre. In the centre hole was a long stick with a socket for the candle at one end and peg-holes through the sides, so that it could be raised or lowered at will. In the other six holes were placed pieces of wood hollowed out like a cup, and into each of these was placed a bottle made of very thin glass and filled with water. These bottles acted as strong condensers or lenses, and the 18 girls sat round the table, three to each bottle, their stools being upon different levels, the highest nearest the bottle, which threw the light down upon the work like a burning-glass. In the day-time as many as 30 girls . . . would work in a room about twelve feet square. . . .

The other side of the lust for lace was an almost unimaginable extravagance. Although the cycle of lace's popularity was volatile, and periods of great excess were peppered with attempts at severe restraint, the edicts and laws, bans and decrees were largely ignored.

Vying for the attention of the reigning monarch, members of the court would try to upstage one another. Their demands for more and more elaborately detailed and inventively ornamented laces escalated beyond their income. Mercurial in their tastes, the aristocratic parasites were notorious, too, for reneging on pay-

At the turn of the century, my husband's grandmother's cousin, Condict W. Cutler, Jr., sat for his portrait amidst a set of Victorian laces.

ment for their laces, and for rejecting laces ordered months in advance simply because a design or pattern had become passé.

So-called sumptuary laws were enacted periodically to stamp out such "excesses of luxury" and to halt outrageous expenditures on items such as lace (which could, and often did, consume a nobleman's entire treasury). During the reign of Edward III in England, for instance, the government enacted a sumptuary law, in 1363, to prohibit the "excessive luxury of veils," and a century later trimmings described as laces were outlawed in a similar edict.

In France, a sumptuary law was decreed by Henry IV in the late sixteenth century as a reaction to the extravagance displayed by his predecessor, Henry III, who had worn, states Mrs. Palliser, "on his own dress, four thousand yards of pure gold lace." Henry IV tried, briefly, to set a prudent example in his own dress, wearing clothes devoid of trim, but his attempts were scoffed at by a class-conscious court who did not want to relinquish their visible tokens of status. Then, reneging on his own edict, he commissioned a high starched ruff to hide a disfiguring scar on his neck. Soon the entire aristocracy of France—and the rest of Europe—followed suit; he thus established a fashion trend that would last for decades. Over time, the ruff, consuming many yards of pleated and starched lace, became more and more extreme until the wearer could hardly turn his or her head. In its way, the ruff was a form of extravagance as extreme as a gold-trimmed suit.

Eventually discomfort forced the demise of the ruff, which was supplanted by the falling collar, obviously softer and easier to wear. The falling collar also re-

A lacemaker's pillow, from Bavaria, is accentuated with angel collages, and several dozen bobbins hang from its pricking.

vealed the delicacy and design of fine lace to greater advantage; falling collars were complemented by cuffs and handkerchiefs, and by tunics and even decorative treatments attached to shoes.

Although women's fashionable attire included lace-embellished bodices, aprons, and lappets, or streamers, hanging from bonnets and headdresses, men actually wore more lace than women throughout the heyday of lace. Especially during the seventeenth century, men sought new ways to incorporate lace into their dress to compete with their peers. During the reign of Louis XIII of France (1610–1643), the scheming Cardinal Richelieu actually encouraged excessive spending on laces and other luxuries by the nobles as a way to exercise control over the court. Courtiers in debt were easier to manipulate to his will. The Queen Regent, in a political ploy, attempted to ban gold and silver embroideries as excessive, but because of Richelieu's power, her bid for circumspection was ignored. Political infighting resulted in edict after edict, but all for naught. In mid-century Louis XIV was ushered as King into a court-condoned atmosphere of great extravagance, which Louis, calling himself the Sun King, did little to dispel. Any dress codes he established were used to set himself apart from, and above, the rest of society; he could ignore any ban himself. Louis's reign, in fact, is acknowledged to be one of exaggerated conspicuous consumption, on a par with that of William and Mary in England (1689–1702) who, after Elizabeth I (1558–1603), were unrivaled in their insatiable appetite for lace.

Louis and his minister Colbert noted, however, that because large quantities of lace were being imported from abroad, monies for their purchase were exhausting the coffers of the court. Also, as partial settlement of a long-term conflict with Spain, Louis had married Marie Thérèse, daughter of Philip IV. Her dowry was enormous, and, after her father's death in 1665, Louis sought to recoup his financial losses by laying claim to lacemaking areas under Spanish domain, notably in the land now called Belgium. Louis banned the import of lace and decreed that all laces worn at Versailles come from his newly instituted Royal Manufactories of Lace.

Laws prohibiting imports typically backfired. Even when the death penalty was invoked to prevent the importing of lace,

ingenuity—and greed—usually won out. Shrewd and devious entrepreneurs resorted to smuggling to ensure a steady source of lace for desperate courtiers.

$\mathcal{M}$rs. Palliser describes one ship, "laden with Flanders lace, bound for England in 1678 . . . The cargo comprised 744,953 ells of lace, without enumerating handkerchiefs, collars, fichus, aprons, petticoats, fans, gloves, etc. . . ."

One popular ploy was quite inventive:

> . . . At one period much lace was smuggled into France from Belgium by means of dogs trained for the purpose. A dog was caressed and fed at home, fed on the fat of the land, then after a season sent across the frontier, where he was tied up, half-starved and ill-treated. The skin of a bigger dog was then fitted to his body, and the intervening space filled with lace. The dog was then allowed to escape and make his way home, where he was kindly welcomed with his contraband charge. These journeys were repeated till the French Customs House, getting scent, by degrees put an end to the traffic. Between 1820 and 1836, 40,278 dogs were destroyed, a reward of three francs being given for each. . . .

Periods of religious persecution also affected the manufacture of lace. When Louis XIV revoked the Edict of Nantes in 1685, for example, setting off sprees of persecution of non-Catholics, he forced thousands of Protestants to flee—including lacemakers. Over four thousand lacemakers escaped Alençon and his Royal Manufactory of Lace located there to Protestant Holland and England where they could practice their religious beliefs—and take up their craft—in a tolerant climate.

The peregrinations of lacemakers, either by choice, by offers of employment, by escape from persecution, or even by kidnapping, has confused the study of lace. One of the reasons laces can be so difficult to identify, either by place or date, is that, as a result of both smuggling and emigration, many supposedly secret lace techniques and designs were reworked, adapted, or simply imitated in a new locale. In Louis XIV's own Royal Manufactories, Italian laces were copied and then given the new name "points de France." Conversely, Alençon-type lace has been found, and made, in Italy, England, and elsewhere.

Civil wars and economic crises erupted sporadically and cast their inevitable influence as well. But it was the Seven Years War of 1756 to 1763, and ultimately the French Revolution, which finally changed fashion, and with fashion, the taste for lace. The elimination or weakening of monarchies, the demise of the aristocracy, and the rise of the bourgeoisie, signaled the end of the heyday of handmade lace. Lace

so visibly symbolized ostentation that the indulgence of its manufacture could not be tolerated. By then, too, men had lost interest in wearing lace. From this time on, despite several revivals of interest, the desire for lace has never again been able to dictate the vagaries of lifestyle as obsessively as it did from the sixteenth through the eighteenth centuries.

After the French Revolution, Napoleon Bonaparte attempted to revive the lace industry in Alençon and Chantilly by virtue of his imperial patronage. He personally sponsored the fabrication of bedhangings, coverlets, and pillowslips of Alençon lace, originally as a gift to Josephine. They were eventually completed in time for his second marriage, to the Empress Marie Louise of Austria, in 1810. This set, emblazoned with lilies and Napoleon's signature bee, are remarkable for their delicacy and precision of design.

But Napoleon's influence over the handmade lace industry, like his tenure as Emperor, was short-lived. The Industrial Revolution, already stirring during his reign, flowered less than a generation after his exile, and irrevocably altered the manufacture of lace. The invention of the loom, a machine capable of producing lace in volume, pushed the already foundering handmade lace industry to near extinction. The twenty-ton Levers machine, invented in 1813 by John Leavers in England—and

A snip of lace (and baby's bonnet) on a front door emulate an old Dutch custom of announcing a birth.

and Mechlin in Belgium. At last, the purchase of lace did not require the income of a nobleman. Now that lace was finally affordable, thousands of enthusiastic middle-class buyers sought it to embellish their clothing and to enhance their decor.

Before the advent of the loom, it had been difficult to render laces in great widths; to create wide pieces, matching lengths of lace had to be meticulously stitched together at their seams. Now laces of all sizes and shapes could be made for apparel and the home.

Although historical mention of household laces occurs in documents such as inventories or bills of sale, few examples predating the nineteenth century have survived —probably because of use and wear—and so it is impossible to speculate on how extensively laces were used throughout the home before the Victorian era. Lace historians have discovered household lists that allude to a variety of uses, from bedcurtains and valances to bedcovers and pillow-slips, from linens for the table to articles for the "toilette." Such lavish ensembles had, of course, cost vast amounts in terms of time and money, and, like fashionable apparel, had not been available to everyone.

The speed and efficiency of machine manufacture spawned such unforeseen luxuries as curtains and tablecloths in great volume. The use of cotton thread, available

just one of myriad lacemaking machines, or looms, developed during the nineteenth century—weaves a total of about three thousand threads to produce a web 224 inches wide and twelve yards long. The design of the lace is controlled by the jacquard, a chain or belt of tied-together punched cards named for their inventor, the Frenchman Joseph-Marie Charles Jacquard. As the loom propels the thread, the thread passes through the card when a hole appears; it is deflected where there is no hole.

By mid-century, designers utilizing such looms proved that handmade lace could frankly be imitated, in versions so precisely rendered that no one except a textile expert could tell the difference —or even particularly cared to. Machine-made laces came to be identified with the names of the lace centers that had once met the demand for handmade lace: Alençon and Valenciennes in France, for instance, or Brussels

20

after the 1830s and less expensive than linen, brought the price of machine lace down still further.

The first Great Exhibition of 1851 in Hyde Park, London, and subsequent international expositions held periodically throughout the latter part of the nineteenth century, showcased, among other decorative arts, extraordinary laces, such as a pair of elaborately detailed curtains manufactured by machine in Nottingham. These expositions sparked a revival of interest in lace, which was also inspired in England by Queen Victoria's own love of lace. She had commissioned locally made Honiton lace to adorn her well-publicized wedding finery in 1840; on the occasion of her Jubilee forty-seven years later she wore a veil, apron, and collar of elaborate appliqué lace combining machine and handmade techniques. During the era spanned by her reign, no bridal ensemble was complete without a veil and lace embellishments on the gown, and no trousseau was complete unless it comprised several sets of bed and table linens bordered with lace.

Handmade laces were also displayed at the great expositions. Viewed by thousands of awestruck spectators, they stimulated a renewed interest in the art and craft of making lace as a hobby. Some of the old pattern books were reprinted, and, once again, rich patrons began to commission specific laces for their homes. Robber baron J. P. Morgan in New York collected laces from the island of Burano, near Venice. New schools, some based in famous lacemaking centers such as Bruges in Belgium and Le Puy in France, revived their old designs. Some of these lace centers still exist today—though their laces are sold mainly to the tourist trade.

What the Victorians called the "gentle arts"—lacemaking, crochet, tatting, and knitting—swept into vogue during the latter part

A stamp set from Spain celebrates the art of lacemaking.

of the nineteenth century, both to enhance clothing and accessories, and because they were considered charming homey pursuits worthy of gentlewomen. Laces for home and toilette seemed limitless in their variety. Antimacassars protected upholstery from hair oil. Doilies dallied under teapots and on muffaneers. Napkins matched up with breakfast cloths, teacloths, and dinner cloths. Pillow cases were made in many sizes.

As laces were again admired, even in countries with weak lacemaking traditions, such as the United States, lace enthusiasts

formed societies and associations to share their interest. Some of these groups, functioning as missionary societies, took it upon themselves to teach lacemaking as a source of income to those they considered less fortunate.

At this time, old laces were honored once more. Some, however, were brought out of storage only to be cut and remade into pieces more suited to contemporary fashion. Others luckily were collected specifically to be preserved intact as remarkable examples of time-honored craftsmanship.

As a result of the impact of the two world wars and the Depression, lace slipped into decline once more. Now, in the 1990s, nostalgia for the gentler lifestyle romantically associated with the Victorians has spawned a renewed enthusiasm for lace. Many shops have sprung up to sell antique and newly made laces, and machine laces are being produced in vast quantities, both as yardgoods and as ready-made home furnishings, such as curtains, tablecloths, and bedcovers.

With love and attention, laces and lace-embellished linens will enhance a table, bed, shelf, or chairback. Newly made machine laces, many crafted from resilient fibers such as natural/synthetic blends—combining cotton with polyester, for example—can hang at the window or from a bed-canopy with little fear that they will fall apart or rot. Handmade lace's so-called cousins—the lacy textiles known as Battenberg lace, Carrickmacross, Limerick lace, and Irish crochet, as well as tatting, filet work, eyelet, and cutwork—all prove suitable for use in home decoration.

Antique handmade laces, however, are now an endangered species; few examples can be found that predate the nineteenth century. Prone to natural decay and disintegration, existing early laces should be carefully stored and not used at all, except on rare occasions for display. Very fine old pieces, in fact, are best consigned to museums, and the meticulous supervision and care of scrupulous curators.

If you want to decorate with old, but not antique, lace, you should, of course, respect its value and its fragility. Caring for old laces and linens requires a commitment of time and effort. Because of this many people shun linens and laces they have inherited. But not using linens and laces may actually hasten their deterioration. Lace, like silver, should be enjoyed; because lace is a living textile it should be allowed to breathe. Less-valuable and brand-new pieces, of course, can be used with less caution. But whatever laces you choose to live with—old or new—love them well. If lace is used because it is loved, and loved because it is used, then that, after all, is what matters most.

A collection of antique lace strips found in an attic are unfolded for inspection as to their condition.

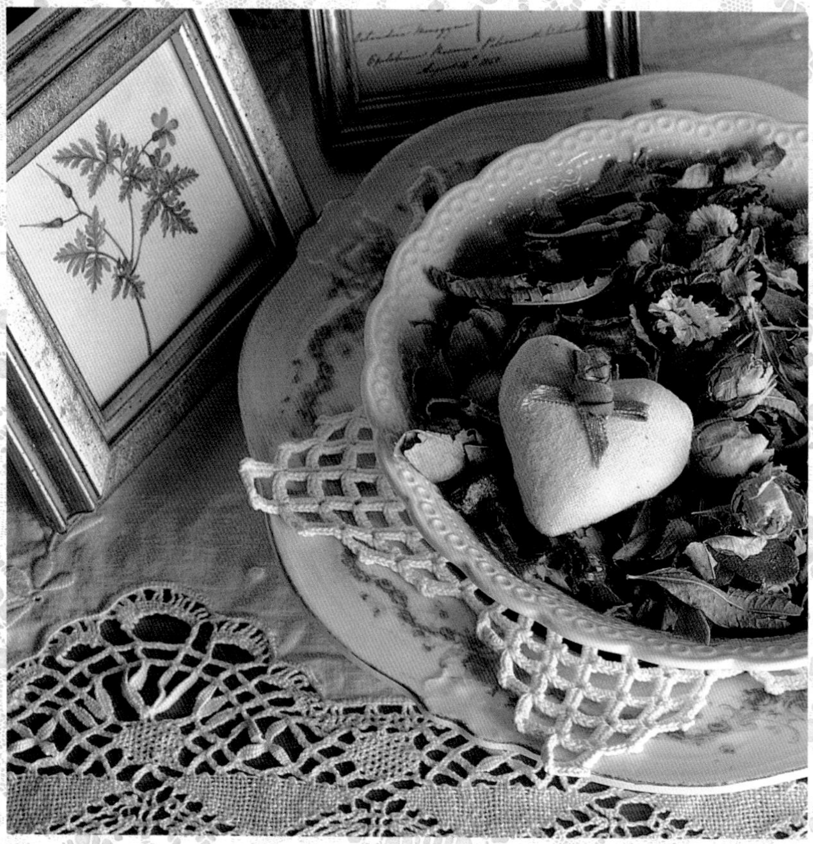

THE LOVE OF LACE

*J*ust what is it about lace that holds us in thrall? When I married, I wore my great-great-grandmother's lace mantilla and carried my great-great-great-grandmother's lace fan. I cherished the web of connection, lace-like in its tenacity, to my ancestors. At home, after my marriage, I accented our rooms with lace, especially lace-embellished bed and table linens, which we had also inherited. ∾ Laces have, in fact, graced the homes of the aristocracy and the very wealthy since the Renaissance. Few records exist describing how these homes looked, however, perhaps because virtually all antique handmade laces created for home use have been lost to decay. ∾ Only within the last century, sparked in part by the advent of looms which could emulate or imitate hand-made laces, has this gossamer fabric truly become a durable and affordable textile for the home. ∾ Today, lace, as well as crochet and cutwork and other lacy textiles, is enjoying a vogue in home decoration. New laces are being produced in great quantity, and old laces are being saved from oblivion and preserved—to decorate windows, tables, beds, shelves, dresser tops, and lampshades. Laces are being used and enjoyed throughout the house—and even out of doors.

$\mathscr{L}$IVING ROOMS, once known as parlors—for "parler," to talk, in French—or drawing rooms or salons, have traditionally been treated with deference, as formal venues for entertaining and ceremony. Often other, less formal rooms were actually "lived" in, and were thus decorated in a style that was more intimate and welcoming. During the Victorian era, it was these rooms, rather than the drawing rooms, that received lace more grace-fully. The living room of that period was suffocated under layers of heavy, dark fabric, and laces were introduced only as accents, such as antimacassars. Today, living rooms are less often and less em-phatically separated from the rest of the house; and they usually absorb many functions besides entertaining. Laces reside in today's living rooms, in ancillary studies, hallways, and indoor porches or garden rooms, with exquisite tolerance for myriad activities, from conversation to game playing to study to television viewing. Laces, and companion fabrics such as cutwork and Battenberg and mesh-background dotted swiss, complement windows, furnishings, and even a doorway or two. And more valuable small laces, matted and framed and set off as art, may hang upon the wall for all to admire.

*I*n his enchanted and
enchanting garden room conjured from a subterranean cell,
designer Charles Riley framed a lyrical panorama
with an extravagant curtain of Irish crochet
secured with a swashbuckling tassel.
He slipcovered a genteel antique Italian settee
with a Venetian-style needle lace cloth,
fastening it to the frame with ribbons;
one corner of the lace, loosened from its tie,
coquettishly bares the delicate shoulder of the settee.
Another panel of age-mellowed lace
backs a Venetian mirror and, across the room,
a second curtain is tethered by a tape-lace collar
teamed with another tassel.

*Overleaf: Designer Bob Patino's Manhattan living room
doubles as a showroom for displaying objects—
such as a breathtaking antique lace—to clients.*

28

*M*rs. William Astor, self-proclaimed
Queen of American Society, boasted the grandest ballroom in 1890s Newport.
In her "cottage," Beechwood, she reserved a boiserie-paneled recess off the ballroom
for intimate amusements such as chamber music and mah-jongg,
Here, French machine laces tame a lofty window and grace a game table.

Textile conservator Bryce Reveley composed her New Orleans living room
as a venue for musicales. Her lace curtains with Cluny borders are hung only through
Mardi Gras; as the sun intensifies from suave to scorching it damages lace.
A shade at the entry and tape lace atop the pianoforte survive year-round use.

32

*A*s founder
of paper white ltd., a manufacturer of
all-white lace-embellished
linens and apparel,
Jan Dutton lives with her creations
on a day-to-day basis.
In her living room and sunroom,
piles of pillows display
a variety of lacy borders.
Christening and day dresses
flutter from tread to tread
down her stairwell
as a backdrop to family photos.

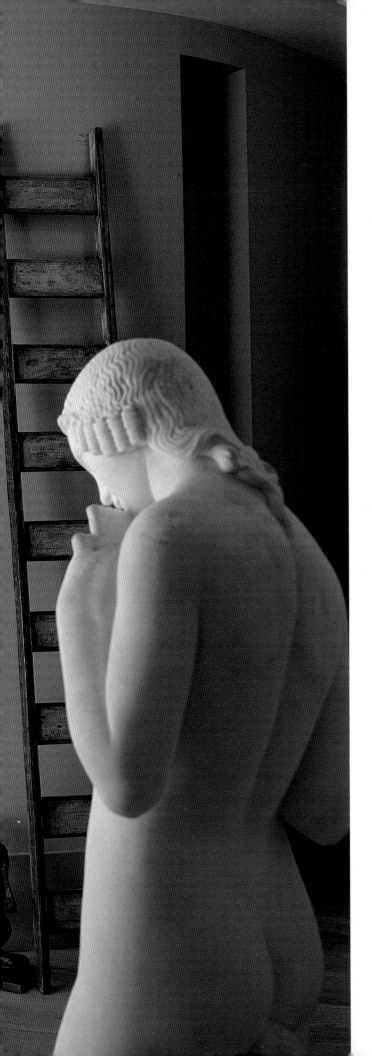

*Anchored by
a post-modern, classically scaled rotunda,
an urbane New York City carriage house
renovated by architect Michael Graves
feels open and airy and, at the same time,
most deliciously intimate.
The soothing color palette and genial proportions
of the interlocking spaces set off a refined melange
of Biedermeier furniture, contemporary artwork,
nineteenth-century statuary, rare books,
and inherited linens and laces.
One lace, a cobwebby mantilla made of wool,
drifts over a silk-upholstered armchair,
solicitous of an evening chill.*

*Overleaf: In their London flat,
magazine editor Anne Hardy and her husband, Jim,
managing director of London's Polo Ralph Lauren shop,
reserve one end of their cozy sitting room
for tea and letter writing. A lace mat
verifies the table's versatility; it can be transformed
from a soft surface for notecards
into an elegant underpinning for a table setting.
A sweetly stitched bertha, a long and lissome collar
Victorian ladies sewed onto their dresses to drape
over their shoulders, accents the wall behind.*

37

A *diminutive patch*
of picot-studded machine lace reclines athwart
a ribbon-tied pinecone wreath.

Well known for her love of collage,
clothing designer Betsey Johnson applied her exuberant gift
for layering color, pattern, and texture
to her country living room; she extends its endearing
embrace with floats of lace at door and window.

40

*A*n industrial loft in Manhattan
is home to designer Vincente Wolf whose sensibility
to seemingly contradictory textures, such as canvas, leather, silk, and lace,
reveals itself in a surprisingly benevolent ambiance.
Wolf wrapped the seat cushion of a gilded bench in a Venetian needle lace
and tossed over another his mother's ethereal wedding veil.

On a hill
in England's lush West Country,
an eighteenth-century orangerie
awaits a presumed entertainment.
The interior is garbed in a dissembling lace:
an ecru veil mantles a graffiti-blazed fireplace
while two complementary laces, a panel and a runner,
drizzle over a table and a Lloyd Loom chair.
Their fragile stitchery blooms are
as detached from reality as those
in the wrought-iron doorstop bouquet.

Overleaf: A filmy tendril of dimestore crochet
is tucked under a mirror, to accentuate
its gilded frame and a pair of old family snapshots.

45

Lots of love
Daisie

*F*or a showcase
in the Place des Antiquaires
in New York City,
the design firm of McMillen, Inc.,
re-created a nineteenth-century
tented Continental library
and placed atop a mahogany table
an elaborate duchesse lace
from Belgium; its medallion detailing
is echoed by another medallion centering
a flower-dappled Aubusson rug.

A designer's desk,
as Charles Riley will attest,
is as much a catchall for inspirations—
a snip of lace, a postcard or two,
harlequin puppets, a ribbon—
as it is a work surface.

Behind a delicately painted
Italian provincial desk
hangs an opulent wallpaper
that mimics elaborately swagged
laces pinioned by rosettes.

*T*ennessee Williams set his play
"Suddenly Last Summer" on the New Orleans porch he frequented in 1941; the porch is now open
for receptions at the invitation of the premier funeral director in town.

Pale-hued furnishings evoke a Swedish influence in a garden room
designed by Barbara Ostrom; she wrapped the sleigh bed's seatcushion in a tablecloth
combining Milanese lace with inserts of point de Venise.

51

*P*hyllis Yes is an artist
based in Oregon who "degenders" objects
by visually altering their surfaces
with patterns based on lace.
Employing an airbrush and then pastry tubes,
she scrolls the lace design upon her chosen object,
be it an epaulet, a Porsche, a handgun—or
a Parsons table used as a desk.

53

$\mathcal{D}$esigner Robert Metzger
tossed an extravagance of blossoms over a tabletop
mantled with an antique silk shawl grandly bordered in lacework
blending filet tirata with point de Venise inserts.
The design of the cascading border echoes the intricacy
of the mother-of-pearl inlays on the sidechairs.

On a fantastical shell-shaped Venetian chair
New Orleans hostess Bethany Bultman
assembled a retrospective still-life that includes a lace collar
that once belonged to her French grandmother,
and which her cousin gave her to wear on her wedding dress.

*P*hotography stylist
Kim Freeman maintains a pied-à-terre
in Manhattan as a studio and workspace.
Antique French lace curtains,
garlanded by trailing ivy,
offset tall windows, and a needle lace,
in a state of semi-decay,
flutters over a lampshade by the sofa.

A strip of dimestore lace
dangling between the pages
of a monogrammed scrapbook keeps track
of long-ago moments in time.

Embossed lace papers were—
and are—often used
as backgrounds for valentines
and other sentimental greetings,
as well as for bouquet papers
and shelf trimming.
Snippets of old lace
may set off photographs in
pretty picture frames.

Overleaf: A sunny corner
in an English manor house invites
a snuggle with a chatty magazine.
The rather formally attired room
acquiesces to an air of nonchalance
by allowing collected laces
to relax at will over the loveseat
as well as at the window.

*L*ight streaming through
a bay window is tempered by a casual cascade of lace.

The V-notched drape of a Bavarian cottage curtain
echoes the rooflines of a birdhouse quartet.

French doors and windows share a southern exposure,
but the impact of the sun is modulated by shutters
pleated over lace panels and matching valances.

Each afternoon,
light billows into the sparely
furnished hallway of
the Isaiah Jones Homestead
bed and breakfast in Sandwich,
Massachusetts, and glances off
a delicately crocheted tablecover
draped handkerchief-style
over the b & b's hall table.
Photographer Norm Darwish,
who coaxes floods of conciliatory light
into his evocative impressions of place,
waited and watched, and waited, to
capture the luminescence in this photo.
He then hand-tinted his image
to bring out the evanescent
complexion of the sun-tinged laces.

63

*A*n infatuation with
the unique engrosses tabletop stylist Linda Cheverton.
In the vestibule of her country house,
a wisp of patchwork constructed of handkerchiefs
conjoined by finespun insertions of lace
languishes over a twiggy bench.
In the dining room, a handknotted and fringed teatowel
domesticates an ecstatic profusion of blossoms
while a reticella-style decorated cocktail napkin,
anchored by a terracotta bowl,
lies quietly alongside a pair of stone figs.

Overleaf: Betsey Johnson brings home leftover chintzes
from her clothing collections to encase bedpillows,
which she then strews at whim—along with window laces—
over a mongrel mix of garden furnishings in her yard.

𝒟INING ROOMS, when set for company, have long been the perfect venue for offering a visual display of the host's esteem and respect for his or her guests. During the heyday of lacemaking, laces used to adorn the table also testified to the extent of one's personal wealth. Early on, therefore, treasured laces were assigned special status as table dressings, and they provided a luxurious backdrop to food and feasting. ∞ Today's formal dining table may still wear a lace-embellished cloth and napery. Informal dining rooms often rely on easy-care, machine-washable laces and lace-bordered linens as underlays for meals taken daily en famille, or for entertaining in a low-key manner. ∞ In the kitchen and pantry, simple and sturdy lace textiles, such as doilies, add wisps of insouciance and charm to otherwise utilitarian settings. Paper lace, and dime-store trimmings, are particular boon companions to the shelf or cupboard, and machine-loomed valances look sprightly at a window or across a passthrough. ∞ Lace tablecoverings enhance outdoor settings, too; who can resist a picnic or a wine tasting under a pergola or trellis, or laid out upon a cutwork cloth on a lawn—or even under the shade of an enormous lace-edged umbrella on a beach?

Of an eve,
my mother will set aside a corner
of her library for a cup of coffee and
a good book. Her table, clouded
in alluring petticoats of lace,
nudges the bookshelves
where a treasured photograph, tiara'd
with a snippet of needle lace,
evokes muse and memory.
The photo recalls a tender moment:
my father toasting my mother—radiant
in lace—at her debutante party,
when they were both seventeen.

70

The Medici
A Great Florentine Family
Balzac
V.S. PRITCHETT
Lorenzo the Magnificent
NANCY
CIVILISATION
Life on Earth
A Portrait of
Marcel Proust
Omega and after
A Proust Souvenir

 beribboned lace veil
swaddles the chandelier in a faux-stone-walled dining room designed by Katherine Stephens
for a high-rise apartment in New York. It recalls the Southern tradition
of secluding best furnishings under cotton or gauze wrappings during the heat waves of summer.

In an elegant parlor in New Orleans, panels of black Chantilly-style lace at the windows
allude to the racy stuff of lingerie, yet exude an aura of grandeur—
in keeping with the lavish, yet intimate, lace-embellished table set for supper "a deux."

$\mathcal{O}$nce an actress,
Virginia Wetherell appreciates and indulges
dramatic settings. To double the height
of her London kitchen—and garner light as well—
she drew an ellipse, freehand, on the floor overhead,
then cut it out and affixed iron fencing all around.
She painted both room and table in misty, pastel shades,
then strewed collected laces here and there as grace notes.
A "four o'clock" teacloth with a filet border
muffles a table in one corner. Grape-cluster lights
sprinkle pale violet orbs of glow—and here her parrot
usually roosts, cackling as Virginia cooks.

Overleaf: A grand linen umbrella,
lacily edged as if by spoondrifts of wave-spray,
shades an Adirondack chair on a rock-studded beach
at the California/Nevada border of Lake Tahoe.
A dip into the water and tip up to the sun ensures that
the purespun linen will remain white all summer.

74

NO
TRESPASSING
VIOLATORS WILL
BE PROSECUTED

Betsey Johnson's
stepback cupboard, crackled like chipped nailpolish,
stashes a whimsical array of ceramics,
some resting upon dainty doilies
that display equally maverick origins and workmanship.
After stripping the kitchen of its claustrophobic knotty pine,
she installed a funky sixty-year-old stove next to a ceramic sink,
then fluttered flea-market petticoat laces at the windows.

Audrey and
Barry Sterling run Iron Horse Winery
in the Alexander Valley in California
as a labor of love, and
their highly praised sparkling wines
have been served in the White House.
Audrey, ever the gracious hostess,
sets up tables for wine tastings
throughout their bountiful gardens—
on terraces, under pergolas
trained with grapevine,
under perfectly pruned shade trees.
She uses scores of laces
and crocheted banquet cloths
collected, like her fine china,
over 38 years of marriage.
Many of her table laces come from
the flea markets in Paris,
where the Sterlings lived for a time.
On the patio behind the house,
a curvaceous wrought-iron table
is diaphanously blurred
with a black Chantilly lace scarf,
its lappets so long they puddle
right onto the ground.

*T*o dress up for a tea,
a rustic side chair and twig table receive slipcovers
of crochet-bordered linen towels
dropped in place with carefree aplomb.

Narrow scalloped lacy trimmings, actually borders cut away
from wide yardage used elsewhere for window curtains,
are folded and tacked beneath open shelves
in the kitchen area of a children's nursery in England.

Overleaf: The contemporary surround
of brick walls and polished oak floors
belies the romantic mood of a Manhattan dining room.
The owners' collection of antique lace doilies
is the perfect foil for Michael Graves' circular table.
The circles-upon-circles of lace also reinforce
the swirling impressions made by paintstrokes
in three numerical studies by artist Jasper Johns.

*A pair of gently pulled lace curtains
and a pillowed window seat lend softness to the corner of a porch.*

*Set for tea, a lace-covered table adds an airy touch to a pretty sunroom.
Lace panels, placed partway up the windows, counterbalance light with privacy.*

ᗷ*ouquets of everlastings,*
swagged with an antique French pindotted mesh ribbon,
dangle like soft stalactites along the ceiling beam
over a fireplace inhabited by a butterfly winged heater.
An English hand-crocheted runner is suspended
from the lip of the fireplace mantel
as an ethereal echo to exuberantly painted swirls.
Behind the pantry door, hooded in filet-work,
lurks the steadfast fridge.

Another mantel, in Florida,
snags a crocheted heart on two talon-tipped hooks
in a floaty gesture of affection.

Overleaf: A doll-sized tea set collects atop a strip
of dimestore crochet on a whitewashed beam.

91

$\mathcal{W}$hite-painted sidechairs
and a scrubbed-pine wall cabinet allude to the Scandinavian
inclinations of a dining area in the home of Lyn Peterson,
founder of a wallpaper and fabric concern called Motif Designs.
A lacy valance decorated with fruits sets off the view
to the backyard behind the house.

94

*In a pre-war building
in Manhattan, a dining room was designed by Cullman & Kravis
to highlight a rare set of Chinese wallpaper panels
dating from the 1770s. Dinner parties in this elegant room
are set on an antique Venetian lace tablecloth
that the owners received as a wedding gift.*

*A fantasia room
contrived for a seductive tête-à-tête
was tented by designer Noel Jeffrey
in an alluring fairytale blue.
Fillips of lace hold tender secrets:
who is vanishing behind the curtain?*

*Antiques dealer Vince Mulford
converted a wartime barracks into a
cottage, where his great-grandmother's
crocheted tablecloth now resides.*

*Practicing his bold yet restrained
mode of decoration,
Robert Currie dresses a refined table
simply with flowers and cutwork cloth.*

97

An old cottage,
transanted from the coast of Maine to California,
was whitewashed throughout to brighten it up.
Lengths of Cluny-style lace trim
accent beams and cupboard shelves in the kitchen,
and dressertop runners attached to curtain rods
function as valances at the window.
A canvas floorcloth was painted, exactly to scale,
to emulate a pillowsham decorated with Bruges lace.

*O*ne log house
on a farmstead north of Oslo, Norway,
is called the "elhuset," or firehouse, because it
harbored the farm cookstove for over eighty years.
Now the cabin, scattered with decorative lacy textiles
to soften its rustic demeanor, serves as a guest dwelling.
Crisply scissored cutwork trim, snipped from paper,
lines shelves and imparts a festive air
to a kitchen cupboard in a cabin in Finland.

99

*V*irginia Wetherell's kitchen
hoards a colorful panoply of antique dinnerwares tucked in
among everyday essentials such as sugar, tea, salt, and semolina.
Taking a cue from her Victorian ancestors,
Virginia caps containers that may entice pesky intruders
with thickly stitched crocheted "flycovers."
Bordered with ball fringe or ornamental roses,
the flycovers are weighted so they won't slip loose of their moorings.

100

*Samantha
escorts her teddy bear to tea,
set out upon a wicker table
topped with a Battenberg hanky.
Always the accomplished hostess,
she never forgets to furl her lace fan
before biting into a single petit four.
After tea, she allows her head
to rest against a diminutive doily
coerced into service to function
as an antimacassar.*

103

$\mathcal{P}$itched among
the outstretched branches
of a gracious and empathetic treetop,
a weathered wooden treeseat,
designed and constructed by British
forestry consultant Richard Craven,
is banked with torchon-trimmed pillows
in anticipation of a drinks party.

Overleaf: A lace-skirted bride
and her groom, freshly transplanted
from the top of a wedding cake,
gaze into their future from a kitchen shelf
trimmed in machine-punched paper lace.

105

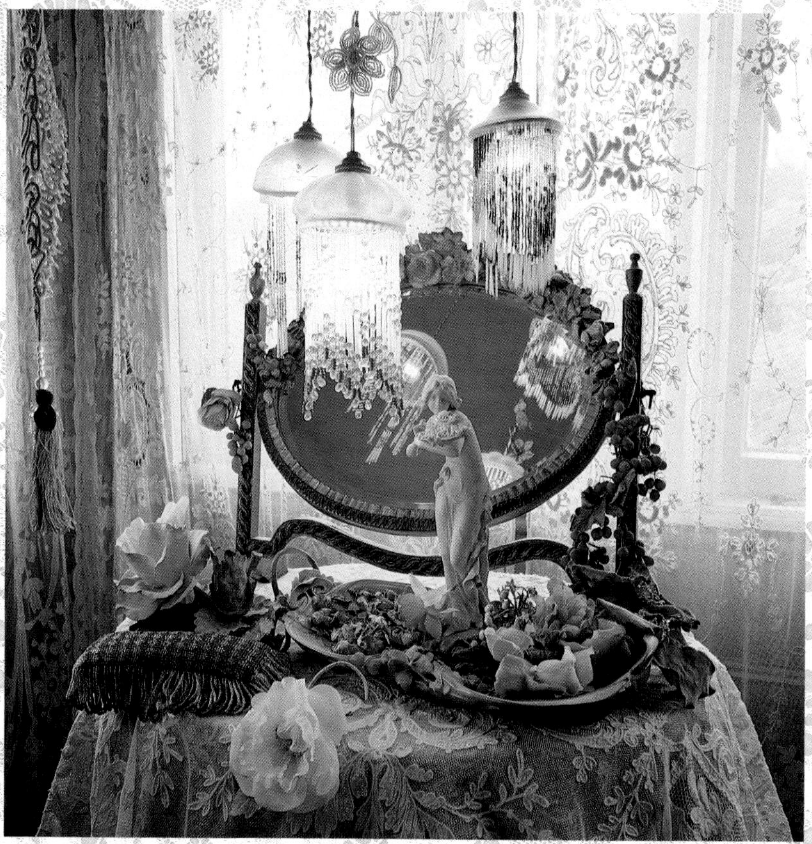

THE LOVE OF LACE

*B*EDROOMS, of all rooms in the house, insist on their entitlement to the wearing of lace. Bed-sheets, cases, and bed hangings crafted of lace, or of lace-enriched linen, have been documented for centuries, as have lacy accoutrements for dressing chambers. Because of their allure lace-endowed bedrooms, dressing rooms, and baths, have often been subjected to the clichéd assertion that because the laces that adorn them serve typically as tokens to romance, they must, of course, be rooms only for seduction—and why not, for lace is, without doubt, the most deliciously romantic of all textiles. ✑ Today, the bedroom—bower or boudoir—still wears lace with tenderness and assurance. Delicate handkerchief linens bordered all around with lace may encase pillows of every shape and persuasion. Tossed about or ranked in polite rows, they will transform any bed into a most beguiling nest. ✑ Bedlinens embellished with lace prove equally enticing in a child's room, especially the nursery, where the delicacy of a lacy design matches the very softness of a baby's skin. ✑ The bathroom, that most private of sanctuaries, coddles fantasy when curtained in lace or fitted out with macrame-fringed or lace-edged towels, and tub and vanity might be petticoated in lace as well.

$\mathcal{W}$ay back in
the recesses of her mother's attic,
illustrator Nelle Davis discovered a box
full of narrow antique lace trimmings
collected by her grandmother to garnish lingerie.
Some of the 1920s lingerie laces
now frolic over window sashes
and across a casually draped curtain.
They blush pale pink, peach, and violet
in the limpid light showering the bedroom
of the riverside cottage Nelle escapes to on weekends
with her husband, photographer Ben Rosenthal.

111

*L*avish lace bedcurtains, wallpaper,
and puffy duvet are hallmarks of an opulent Lord & Taylor bedroom scheme.

A restored Dutch colonial cottage displays restraint and reserve,
except that the centered bed is set askew. Scandinavian-inspired bedding is layered
with a crisp embellished linen twinsheet for textural contrast.

For an Alabama Symphony Orchestra Showhouse, designer Maurine Abney
hung translucent filet-work directly from the eave rather than only in the window.

A bead-encrusted pelmet
is just one of myriad French and English laces
Virginia Wetherell has collected over twenty years,
both for her antiques shop in central London
and for her peach-toned bedroom.
Using machine-net curtains decorated with tapework,
she sewed up a sweeping half-tester to float
like a cloud over her late Victorian brass bed.
The linen topsheet was finished off with a deep border
of crochet; all pillows, from the 1920s, are French.

Overleaf: Vincente Wolf works out daily in his
north-facing bedroom, attended by a lace-scrimmed and
soundless stela of television monitors
tuned in to Channel 66, the channel of perpetual snow.
The designer vaulted another lace across his window
and into a compliant billowing silk drapery.

114

*R*esting against the arches
of an imaginary loggia, a quilt-and-lace gowned chaise
recuperates from the debaucheries of Mardi Gras in the early morning sun.
A flit of lacy trim reins in the louvred shutters
to prevent eddying breezes from slamming them to and fro.

118

*O*nce consecrated as a chapel,
Bethany and Johann Bultman's New Orleans' bath still proudly wears
its original filigreed wrought-iron churchgates.
A Victorian-style machine lace curtain, backed with plastic,
hangs at the shower to prevent stray drops from pooling on the tiled floor.

119

*F*riends staying the night
in Betsey Johnson's country house are treated to the loveliness of laces
flung like fragile kerchiefs over an iron bedstead.

Inspired by the richness of tapestry, Charles Riley created
a boudoir dense with texture, jewel-tone color, and pattern.
A glorious length of Irish crochet, with an astonishing "finger" border,
cowls an elaborate screen, while an airier lace, a bureau scarf,
stands in for an antimacassar on a leaf-emblazoned loveseat.

*ntique bedlinens
culled from flea markets in Paris
proffer nocturnal reminders
of sojourns in France.*

*In a California nursery,
Goldilocks and the Three Bears
join up with pillows to guard baby.*

*Even dolly and her teddy may recline
against a lace-edged pillow.*

*H*eirloom lace
and crochet accent a window and
bedtable in a room setting
designed to highlight
the Ralph Lauren Home Collection.

Lace entrepreneur Pam Kelley
likens the boldly stitched
machine-lace curtains
hanging in her Newport guestroom
to "grandmother's lace"
because they remind her of handiwork
found in flea markets in France.

A guest bedroom
in a cottage in northern California
is cleverly curtained with
a cutwork-trimmed linen apron.

Overleaf: When Lyn Fabacher
converted a cramped two-room study
in her New Orleans home
into a master bath, she was able to save
and restore an antiquated clawfoot tub
and center it in the new space.
Instead of a bathmat, she slung
a filet-work teatowel over its rim.
A deeply fringed lace valance,
aged to the color of café-au-lait,
drapes a mantel she pickled and
positioned between shuttered windows.

*S*ometimes
it is just one single lacy effect,
such as a neatly folded handkerchief,
that draws the eye
to a beautiful collection.

On my parents' dresser,
family mementoes include a miniature
sterling silver bed that was
a 25th anniversary gift,
now canopied with a tendril of lace.

A tea towel,
laid sideways to reveal its
zigzaggy filet border,
sets off best pals Tom and Huck.

Dropped onto an oval lace mat
in my mother's dressing table,
lie personal heirloom treasures,
including a needle-lace-and-ivory fan,
which belonged to my great-great-great-
grandmother, and a Cinderella slipper.

*T*o showcase
a bedding line for J. P. Stevens,
stylist Stanley Hura
designed a whitewashed cabin
and filled it with a charming
and eclectic mix of furnishings.
Inventive bedhangings
were contrived from yards
of restaurant-issue cheesecloth.
Dimestore lace trim
encircles the curvy iron washstand
and a flowerpot,
while another snip of lace rests
in an abandoned bird's nest.

Overleaf: A diaphanous nightshift,
accented with lace and monogrammed
with the letters M. R. S.
in acknowledgment
of its owner's marital status,
hangs, after washing,
in the sunset's shimmery glow.

130

$\mathscr{A}$s a jewelry designer,
Mignon Faget sensitizes herself to the elemental shapes
and textures of the Louisiana bayou that inform her creations.
Analogous sympathies inspire her New Orleans home. Her bedroom is a bower
at once magical and sensual, with voodoo figures and masks sharing wall and bed
with romantic laces, including a diaphanous Normandy spread,
and precious passementerie. Her "Zia" bracelets and rings adorn a pair of porcelain
glove forms on the mantel, poised atop an antique flounce of lace.

134

tower bedroom
soaring above a suburban house designed by Noel Jeffrey
was fitted out with a dark wood suite
inspired by the furnishings of Charles Rennie Mackintosh.
Jeffrey drew a vast sweep of Nottingham lace
across the bay window, both to filter light
and to sprinkle pointillist sparkles of sun into the room.

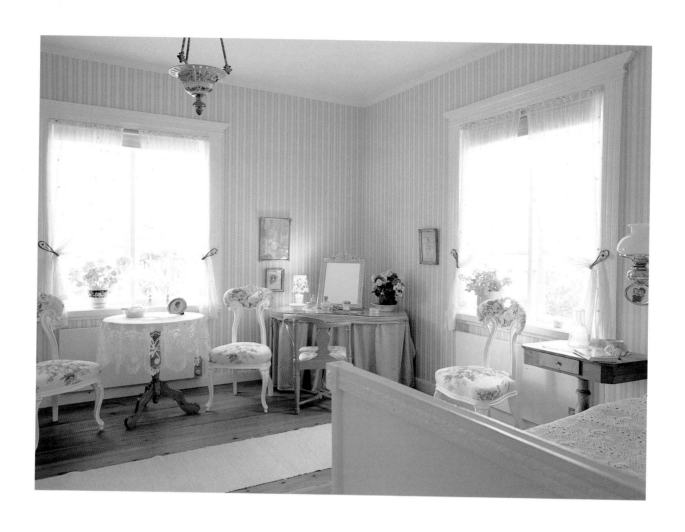

*I*n a weekend retreat
in Finland, an exquisite bedroom with striped walls
contests the often gloomy climate with generous doses of light
and pretty white-painted furnishings
that date from the eighteenth and nineteenth centuries.
A cache of Russian laces found in the attic
was used throughout the room, and throughout the house.

137

*T*he sponge-painted clawfoot tub
in Virginia Wetherell's London bathroom once stood, full of coal,
by a roadside in France. Virginia cleaned it up and draped it
with a filet-bordered towel in lieu of a mat.
The 1880s' French tape-work lace she hung as a valance in the window
is called a portico because it would once have accentuated a doorway.

Jan Dutton's marble-clad bathroom in northern California reverberates
with morning sun. Cutwork-decorated paper white curtains and valances framing tub
and window hang directly from the ceiling for an illusion of extra height.

139

A French
machine lace tablecloth,
accentuated by medallion motifs,
rests atop an arched canopy
on the bed belonging to
Pam and Brendan Kelley, owners
of the Rue de France lace shop
in Newport, Rhode Island.

Overleaf: Light diffuses into
a sleeping porch in Michigan
through pieces of tracing paper
inset over the windowpanes.
Linda Evans, a designer
and a mother, made the layette
from remnants of antique laces,
including filmy shreds
from damaged wedding dresses.

140

$\mathcal{D}$esigning an atelier
for a worldly couple—a composer and a dancer—
and their new baby, Feldman • Hagan Interiors
sympathetically catered to their artistic leanings
by expansively embracing within the room
a piano, a ballet barre, a chess set, and a crib—
as well as an antique Spanish bed, draped in lace,
raised on a dais in one corner under the eave.

144

$\mathcal{W}$hat Bethany Bultman
calls her "summer spread"—a flounced frivolity of net
appliqued with Brussels lace—falls in flourishes
over an enormous mahogany fourposter bed
in her high-ceilinged New Orleans guestroom,
and is often teamed up with a mosquito netting canopy.
The tripartite screen was designed to display
nineteenth-century lace panels and strips.

145

*I*n a dressing room in San Francisco,
a mirror, mantilla'd with lace, gazes benignly upon a flirtatious camisole.

Jessica McClintock, renowned for her luscious lacy ballgrowns
and wedding dresses, used lavish amounts of lace
throughout her home in northern California.
Even an overscaled third-floor shower room received frothy curtains.

Overleaf: After tripping the light fantastic,
a pair of pink lace stockings cool out over a jalousie window in Key West.

PLEASE NOTE THIS
PRODUCT IS REDEEMABLE
AGAINST PURCHASES
MADE THROUGH
CATHERINE BUCKLEY
OUTLETS ONLY

THE LOOK OF LACE

*G*ossamer-fine and delicate as a cobweb, lace belies an unusual tensile strength. For this reason many pieces of lace have survived longer than other less resilient textiles.

Thousands of laces, however, have been lost. Sumptuary laws, which periodically banned lace as an unacceptable symbol of material excess, caused many extraordinary laces to be burned or destroyed. Still others languished in storage and fell victim to mildew and decay; others were used until they turned into rags.

Until the Industrial Revolution made machine-spun laces available to a general and enthusiastic public, laces had been commissioned only by the very wealthy. They were generally consigned to the care of then-professional "lace-washers," who specialized in washing, bleaching, starching, and pressing lace. Because of this conscientious care, many of the aristocratic laces that reside in museum collections appear as crisp and lustrous as they did when new.

Today, with correct handling and storage, you too should be able to preserve your laces for generations to come.

Caring for antique laces

If you believe your lace to be antique, especially if it is handmade and over 100 years old, it is best to entrust its cleaning and repair —and restoration, if necessary and desired—to a conservator. The field of textile conservation is growing, especially as more and more people collect antique textiles. Because many conservators are affiliated with museums, consult the museum nearest you to see if it can locate a conservator in your area.

In Bryce Reveley's Gentle Arts studio in New Orleans, a trained seamstress repairs and restores a wedding veil.

You may also contact the three universities that offer degrees in textile conservation: the University of Delaware in conjunction with Winterthur Museum; the University of North Carolina; and New York University. In addition, the American Institute of Conservation or the Costume Society of America might be able to recommend an expert in the field.

The conservator's role is to stabilize the present condition of the textile so that it will not deteriorate further. By contrast, a restorer will try to return an antique textile to its original condition. If a lace is in a state of severe deterioration, it may not be able to endure restoration without further damaging the fragile fibers.

Caring for new machine-made lace

New machine-made laces of cotton, linen, polyester, or a blend may be washed following their enclosed instructions, if any, or in the washing machine. Use a gentle cycle and a gentle soap such as Ivory soapflakes. Such laces may also be machine dried, preferably on a tumble-dry, no heat cycle. Many new linens that are embellished with lace require handwashing and line-drying, or must be dried, like a sweater, blocked upon a towel. Check the manufacturer's instructions for the recommended procedure. Do not send lace or lace-embellished linens to a dry cleaner as the solvents used are too harsh; commercial laundries, too, may submit delicate linens to undue stress.

How to wet-clean lace

Wet-cleaning is a soak-and-rinse process that allows lace to be thoroughly cleaned with a minimum of handling and agitation and can be used for any fine lace, old or new, that should not be machine-washed. Hand-washing, which entails rubbing and tumbling and wringing, can damage fine lace.

Be sure to set aside enough time

to clean lace. Soaking lace can take up to an hour or more, as can rinsing, and drying can take even longer.

Before cleaning your lace, assemble all your materials and wash out the interior of your sink or basin, removing any grease or soapy residue that could be transferred to the wet lace.

Natural fibers, especially those in antique textiles, weaken under the stress of the extra weight of moisture; the fibers—be they linen or cotton or even wool—can stretch and possibly tear. Therefore, lace must be supported while it is wet. It is recommended that you use a framed nylon screen, the kind used to wash and block sweaters, if it will fit inside your sink without tipping. Having the screen in the sink should not inhibit an easy flow of water down the drain, and it should be easy to lift the screen out of the sink without jarring the lace.

If you do not have a framed nylon screen, you can use a clean, but not new, white or pale-colored cotton towel instead. Fold the towel lengthwise so that it will lie flat in the bottom of the sink from front to back. Draw the ends up over the sides of the sink. Use the ends to lift and lower the lace.

Place the lace gently on top of the screen or towel, so that it lies flat. If the piece of lace is longer or wider than the screen, fold it, but be sure it will lie flat when wet.

You must use tepid, soft, min-

What you will need to wet-clean lace

Stretched nylon screen in frame (the kind used for washing and blocking sweaters)

or

Clean, used, white (or pale-colored, if there is no danger of bleeding), 100-percent cotton terrycloth towel

Plastic dishpan (optional)

Pure distilled water

or

Charcoal-filtered, soft tap water

Mild soap or cleaning solution recommended for fine textiles, such as liquid Lavant or LeBlanc Linen Wash or Orvus WA Paste or Ivory soapflakes

Hydrogen peroxide or sodium perborate (optional)*

Soft, natural sponge

* Use these lightening agents only if your lace is new and durable and there is no danger of damaging fibers

eral-free water to wet-clean lace; lace can be damaged by hard water. If you cannot filter your water, use pure distilled water, available in gallon jugs, instead. The water should be no hotter than body temperature. Water that is too hot will cause fibers to shrink; water that is too cold shocks the fibers. Never add softeners or other agents to the water.

Most dealers counsel simple soaking, without soap. If you feel you must enlist a soap to hasten cleaning, or to remove soils, try one of the gentle, chemical-free products especially formulated for delicate textiles. (See box above for a list of cleaning products.) Mix one tablespoon of the soap prod-

153

uct into one gallon of tepid water.

A gentle pre-soak of about 10 to 15 minutes, without soap, will establish whether or not the soil on your lace will release easily. Pour in just enough water to cover the lace; too much water may agitate it. If, after the pre-soak, the lace seems to retain too much soil, then drain off the water and refill to cover with a soapy solution in the proportions outlined above. If you need more than a gallon of water to cover the lace, add more water but do not add more soap.

Leave the lace to soak in the soapy solution for 30 minutes. Then lift the screen very carefully to allow the water to run freely through the lace and to ascertain if any soils have been released. As the lace lies flat you can gently dab it with a soft natural sponge to push water through the mesh. Do not press hard on the sponge.

If your lace rests on a towel, drain all water and then press a second towel over the lace to push water through. Then remove top towel and proceed with rinsing.

If your lace is brand-new and sturdy, you may be able to lighten it, if necessary. Hydrogen peroxide or sodium perborate can be diluted five to one in water and added to the soapy solution.

Once the lace appears clean, drain out the water very slowly. If you are using a basin instead of a sink, lift the screen or towel out of the basin and set it flat upon a counter before tipping the water

Gentle Arts studio has an enormous tub that was engineered for wet-cleaning large pieces of lace and other textiles.

155

out of the basin. Never tip lace when it is wet as the weight of the moisture causes stress.

Rinse the lace by allowing water to flow in a gentle and continuous stream into the sink. Do not direct the flow of water onto the lace itself, but run the water continuously for 30 minutes, being sure water covers lace, and then inspect the lace to see if the water is running clear. If not, keep running the water until it does run clear.

If your faucet cannot be maneuvered to the edge of the sink, you will have to fill the sink with enough water to just cover the lace and then proceed as you did for the wet-clean cycle, draining and refilling and draining again a half-dozen times or more until the water runs clear.

When the water is clear, drain it off completely. Then gently blot the lace, while it is still resting flat on the screen in the sink, with a clean, used, cotton terrycloth towel to absorb as much of the residual moisture as possible. Used toweling works best as it will not transfer lint to your lace. Never twist or wring lace.

If you feel comfortable enough with the wet-clean process to handle larger pieces of lace, such as tablecloths, bedcovers, or curtains, you can follow these directions, but work in a bathtub rather than a sink. Set your screen in the bathtub and have enough pure water and soap product at hand to double or even triple the amounts of recommended for smaller pieces.

Fold the tablecloth or bedcover until it can rest on the screen with no extra fabric falling over the edges. Then proceed as above. Because the cloth will be much heavier than a smaller piece, be careful when you attempt to lift the screen during each phase of the cycle. Have plenty of towels on hand to blot the cloth after the final rinse is complete. Allow the cloth or cover to dry out to a comfortable dampness before attempting to block it.

How to dry lace

Lift the lace on its nylon screen or towel and place it on a clean, used, cotton terrycloth towel on a flat surface, such as a countertop, near the sink. Blot the lace with another clean used cotton towel, and keep blotting, to absorb as much residual moisture as possible. Then place the almost-dry lace, as is, on a dry towel on another flat surface, such as a towel-covered tray or screen, or picture frame glass and

---

* What you will need to dry and block lace

Clean, used, white (or pale), 100-percent cotton terrycloth towels

or

Clean, used, white, 100-percent cotton or linen bedsheets or pillowcases, for large items

Homosote, picture frame glass, or sheet acrylic, to rest lace on

Rust-proof straight pins, or kitchen tumblers or jelly glasses

A handkerchief is held in place by stainless steel pins as it is blocked after repair.

set it in a well-ventilated place out of direct sunlight. Ultraviolet rays harm delicate textiles.

If your lace is brand-new and sturdy, you can set it out in the sun and open air to dry.

If the piece is small and easy to manage, you may block it while drying. Press it gently into shape with your fingers and then place kitchen glasses along the edges to hold it flat and steady.

How to block a tablecloth or other large piece of lace

Because a tablecloth, or other large household lace such as a curtain panel or a bedcover, is so large, you will need to prepare a broad surface to spread out the cloth without folding it. A four-foot by eight-foot panel of homosote will work well, but you must cover it tautly with a clean used cotton sheet to protect your lace.

Lay the piece of lace gently on top of the covered homosote and press it flat with your fingers. Using rust-proof straight pins, pin through the holes or mesh of the border of the lace at four-inch intervals. Never pierce the whole-cloth, only the holes, as you do not want to damage the lace. Be sure the lace is pulled tight but not too taut; as it dries the lace fibers become less elastic and will shrink ever so slightly.

If you do not have pins or if you are concerned about using them, you can use kitchen tumblers or glasses instead. Place them at the same intervals around the edge of the cloth.

How to remove common stains from lace

Most common water-soluble stains, including those generated by citrus juices, milk, cream, or egg, can be lifted from lace with a few gentle rinses of tepid water, but only if the stain is fresh and has not begun to dry or set. More stubborn stains should not be treated with home remedies. Send badly stained lace to a conservator experienced in the care of antique textiles.

If the stain covers a very small area, you can support the lace over a tea strainer as you rinse it. This will relieve stress on the dampened fibers. If the stain is larger, place the lace flat on a framed nylon screen in the sink before rinsing.

If your lace is brand-new and sturdy, you may even have luck removing more resistant stains, such as red wine, grease, or candle wax. For red wine, dust the stain immediately with salt or saturate it in club soda, as you would with any linens. For grease, thickly dust the spot with talcum powder. For candle wax, gently scratch the wax with a dull knife and then press absorbent paper against any residue. Follow any of the above treatments with several rinses of tepid water, and then wet-clean or wash the lace, depending upon its value and age.

How to iron lace

Lace will look crisp and fresh and will also be less prone to damage if it is kept free of wrinkles and creases. Soil and mildew can build up inside creases causing the fragile natural fibers to decay.

The safest procedure for eliminating wrinkles in a small and manageable piece of lace is to block the lace, as described above, while it air-dries.

Lace can also be ironed, but only very gently. Lace must be ironed while still damp because dry fibers become brittle and can break under the weight and heat of an iron. Damp fibers are slightly elastic and can tolerate cautious ironing.

If you plan to iron your lace, do not allow it to dry out completely after wet-cleaning. If you want to iron lace that is dry, mist it carefully beforehand until it feels damp but not wet.

Some dealers advocate cooling the lace slightly while it is still damp so that the iron will not overheat the fibers. To do this, fold the damp lace carefully into a plastic bag and place it flat on a shelf in the refrigerator for an hour or two. Be sure not to leave the lace in the refrigerator indefinitely, or even overnight, as the sustained moisture will foster mildew.

Never starch old lace. Starch creates a gummy residue that may damage fibers. Only brand-new and sturdy lace can be starched, but never stiffly.

Inspect your iron and ironing board. To reduce tension on the lace, use an ironing board that has been padded and then covered tautly with a clean used cotton sheet. The iron, too, must be clean. Rinse it thoroughly with a vinegar and water solution to release any mineral build-up. Be sure the soleplate is smooth and free of scorchmarks or starchy residue.

Set your iron on a medium-cool setting. Never use steam. Steam,

---

*** What you will need to iron lace**

Iron, preferably with coated soleplate

Plastic bag (optional)

Ironing board, preferably padded

Clean, used, white, 100-percent cotton sheet, to cover padded ironing board

Clean, used, white, 100-percent cotton terrycloth towel, to pad and protect heavy-textured lace

Pressing cloth, either another clean, used, cotton sheet or a cotton or linen towel usually used for drying crystal

158

A small collection of doilies and hankies is stored between folds of a clean linen sheet in an open basket.

like hot water, can damage fibers, causing them to shrink and tear.

Never iron lace directly. Place the lace face down on the sheet covering the ironing board. Lace looks best when it is not pressed completely flat, so if your lace has a raised pattern or is highly textured, place a clean, used, cotton terrycloth towel underneath to cushion the lace. Cover the lace with a clean pressing cloth; this can be another clean used cotton sheet or a cotton or linen towel usually used for drying crystal or glassware.

Never press too hard on the iron. Keep the iron in motion at all times, using circular sweeps across the pressing cloth. Keep checking, both to see when the lace is neatly pressed and when it is dry. Do not overheat the lace.

If your lace is particularly large —a curtain panel, for example, or a tablecloth—pull up a table alongside the ironing board and transfer each dry section of the lace from the ironing board across to the table. Never let lace pile up or hang from the ironing board.

How to store lace
Lace made of natural fibers— linen, cotton, silk, or a blend of these—must be allowed to

159

breathe. If you bury lace in tight-lidded boxes or trunks or cedar chests it may mildew or rot. Instead, store lace in wide, shallow, open-weave baskets that have never been treated with stain or oil. Acid-free cardboard boxes, capped with loose-fitting lids, are also suitable. Line the baskets or boxes with a layer of clean, used, cotton sheeting or with acid-free archival tissue.

Small laces should always lie flat on the bed of sheeting or tissue. Additional layers of sheeting or tissue should separate individual pieces. A last layer tops them off as a dustcover.

Large laces, such as curtain panels, bedcovers, or tablecloths, should be rolled up on acid-free cardboard tubes, if possible. If acid-free tubes are unavailable, you can use long wrapping-paper tubes, bolt-fabric rollers, or map rollers. Always wrap the roller with a clean, used, cotton sheet and tuck in the ends. If the lace is wider than the tube, fold it length-wise to fit. It is recommended that before you begin rolling, you cover the lace with another clean, used, cotton sheet. Then roll this up with the lace so that it layers and protects it. Roll slowly and carefully on a flat surface to avoid wrinkles. If you are ironing the large piece of lace, you can roll as you go, transferring each ironed section to the adjoining table—and tube.

Store your lace in a cool, dry, dark place away from drafts. Extremes in humidity and temperature may hasten staining, mildew, and rot, so an uninsulated attic or damp basement are poor storage options.

If you plan to store your lace for an extended period of time, take it out occasionally—at least twice a year—to see that it has not started to discolor, a first sign of deterioration. Pull the laces out to air; rest them on a bed overnight, away from children or pets, and then replace them in their baskets or boxes. Refold folded laces to avoid creasing, and rotate the laces, transferring them from top to bottom, bottom to top, in the basket or box.

Never add a cedar block or potpourri; oils in the wood, blossoms, or leaves could stain the lace.

To further protect the basket or box you can wrap and tie it entirely, like a gift package, in a clean, used, cotton sheet. Never wrap in plastic because, as stated at the outset, lace must breathe.

---

* What you will need to store lace

Shallow, open-weave, natural and unstained baskets
or
Acid-free archival cardboard boxes with
loose-fitting lids

Acid-free cardboard tubes

Clean, used, white, 100-percent cotton or linen sheets
and/or pillowcases
or
Acid-free, archival tissue paper

160

DIRECTORY

This directory offers a selection of shops and dealers specializing in antique and new laces. The selection is by no means exhaustive—we recommend that you investigate any local shops or dealers offering antiques and collectibles to ascertain if they also carry laces. Sources for lacemaking supplies, acid-free tubes, boxes, and tissue, and special cleaning agents are also included, as well as a selection of books for those inclined to research the subject of lace, especially its history and technique. A few textile conservators are mentioned, and an international organization whose purpose is to promote interest in lace and lacemaking.

ANTIQUE LACES

. . . AND OLD LACE
320 Court Street
Salem, OR 97301
(also publishes newsletter)

THE ANTIQUE TEXTILE COMPANY
100 Portland Road
London, England W11 4LQ

RUTH ARZT
85 Leewater Avenue
Massapequa, NY 11758
(by written appointment only)

BAZAAR DES BEARS
1909 First Avenue
Seattle, WA 98101

CATHERINE BUCKLEY LTD.
Couturier Dresses & Antique Laces
302 Westbourne Grove
London, England W11 2PS
(by written appointment only)

CHERCHEZ
862 Lexington Avenue
New York, NY 10021

LINDA EVANS REMEMBERS
P.O. Box 413
Trenton, MI 48183

FILIGREE
Antique Linens, Laces, Clothing &
    Accessories
1210 Yonge Street
Toronto, Ontario
Canada M4T 1W1

GOLYESTER
Antique Clothing and Costumes, Lace &
    Linens
1356 Washington Boulevard
Venice, CA 90291

HOME SWEET HOME ANTIEK
799 Grand Avenue
St. Paul, MN 55126

HORSEFEATHERS ANTIQUES
P.O. Box 562
454 Route 6A
East Sandwich, MA 02537

KATY KANE
Antique Clothing & Fine Linens
34 West Ferry Street
New Hope, PA 18938

LACE COLLAGES
88 Lexington Avenue
New York, NY 10016
(pillows made with remnants
of antique laces; by written appointment
only)

LACE LEGACY
Antique Linens & Clothing
220 South First
Kent, WA 98032

LACE WORKS, INC.
with ANN LAWRENCE ANTIQUES
Heirloom Lace, Linens, Clothing &
    Decorative Objects
250 West 39 Street
New York, NY 10018
(by appointment only)

LACIS
2982 Adeline
Berkeley, CA 94703

LADY SYBIL'S CLOSET
Vintage Linens and Laces
1484 Church Street
San Francisco, CA 94131

JULE LANG
255 Audubon Street
New Orleans, LA 70118
(by appointment only)

LAVENDER & LACE
Antique Linens and Lace, Clothing &
    Accessories
656 N. Larchmont Boulevard
Los Angeles, CA 90004

LILACS & LACE
43355 Julian Highway, #780
Santa Ysable, CA 92070

LUCULLUS
610 Chartres Street
New Orleans, LA 70130

LUNN'S ANTIQUES
86 New King's Road
Parsons Green
London, England SW6 4LU

SUE MADDEN
Stand 128
Gray's Antique Market
58 Davies Street
London, England W1

MAISON ANTOINE
OLD BRUSSELS LACE SHOP
Grand' Place, 26
Brussels, Belgium

MOSTLY MEMORIES
Heirloom Lace and Linens, Antique Gifts
5611 Jumilla Avenue
Woodland Hills, CA 91364

NATARA'S COLLECTION
Clothing and Lace
1396 Yonge Street
Toronto, Ontario
Canada M4T 1W1

FRANÇOISE NUNNALLÉ
105 West 55 Street
New York, NY 10019
(by written appointment only)

THE OLDE LACE STORE
Lace-Embellished Clothing & Accessories
12134 Ventura Boulevard
Studio City, CA 91604

PARIS 1900
Vintage Linens & Clothing
2703 Main Street
Santa Monica, CA 90405

REMAINS TO BE SEEN
323½ Lundlow Avenue
Cincinnati, OH 45220
and
9395 Montgomery Road
Cincinnati, OH 45242

JANA STARR/JEAN HOFFMAN ANTIQUES
236 East 80 Street
New York, NY 10021

ROBINSON'S ANTIQUES
1236 Yonge Street
Toronto, Ontario
Canada

TROUVAILLE FRANÇAISE
New York City
212-737-6015
(by appointment only)

LOUISE VERSCHUEREN
Rue Watteau, 16
1000 Brussels, Belgium

VIRGINIA ANTIQUES
98 Portland Road
London, England W11

ELAINE WILMARTH DESIGN
RESOURCES
Antique Linens & Clothing
5715 Sir Galahad Road
Glenn Dale, MD 20769

NEW LACES

ALIX AND ALEXIS
956 Lexington Avenue
New York, NY 10021
(lace-accented accessories)

AMAZING LACE & LINEN CO.
P.O. Box 5406
Richmond, CA 94805
(curtains, bedlinens, tablelinens, doilies,
runners; catalog)

ANICHINI LINEA CASA
Route 110
Tunbridge, VT 05077
(lace-embellished bedlinens, towels,
tablelinens; write for a where-to-buy listing)

LAURA ASHLEY HOME SHOP
714 Madison Avenue
New York, NY 10021
(Nottingham curtains, bedcovers, tablelinens,
yardgoods; write for a where-to-buy listing)
and
LAURA ASHLEY HOME CATALOG
1300 MacArthur Boulevard
Mahwah, NJ 07430

FIONA BARCLAY's
TROUSSEAU OF NOTTINGHAM LACE
(above James Bell Hire)
Woolpack Lane
The Lace Market
Nottingham, England WG1 1GA
(lace-accented tablelinens, pillows,
accessories; catalog)

J. R. BURROWS & CO.
Victorian Design Merchants
P.O. Box 418
Cathedral Station
Boston, MA 02118
(Nottingham curtains, yardgoods; catalog)

THE CLAESSON CO., INC.
P.O. Box 130
Route 1
Cape Nettick, ME 03902
(European curtains, valances, shower
curtains, tablecloths, yardgoods; catalog)

COUNTRY CURTAINS
at The Red Lion Inn
Stockbridge, MA 01262
(curtains; catalog)

DAWN'S EARLY LIGHT
P.O. Box 935
Nyack, NY 10960
(cutwork bed and tablelinens, European
curtains, yardgoods, lampshade covers;
catalog)

LA DENTELLIÈRE
11 Harwood Court
Scarsdale, NY 10583
(European curtains, valances, yardgoods)

KATHA DIDDEL HOME COLLECTION
for Twin Panda, Inc.
420 Madison Avenue
New York, NY 10017
(lace-accented bedlinens, pillows; write for a
where-to-buy listing)

THE GOLDEN APPLE
Metrocenter
49 Court Street
Binghamton, NY 13901
(lace-accented pillowcases, tablelinens,
doilies, runners; catalog)

GAIL GRISI STENCILING, INC.
Lace Division
P.O. Box 1263
Haddonfield, NJ 08033
(curtains, tablelinens; catalog)

JESURUM
San Marco, 4310
Ponte Canonica
Venice, Italy
(lace and lace-accented linens, accessories)

KANTENPARADIJS
8, Rezenhoedkaai
Bruges, Belgium
(lace and lace-accented linens, accessories)

LA LACE SHOP
423 Perrymount Avenue
San Jose, CA 95125
(wholesale and retail)

LACE COUNTRY
21 West 38 Street
New York, NY 10018
(curtains, valances, swags, yardgoods; catalog)

LINEN LADY
885 57 Street
Sacramento, CA 95819
(curtains, tablelinens)

LINENS & LACE
#4 Lafayette
Washington, MO 63090
(Bavarian curtains, valances, bedlinens,
tablelinens; catalog)

LONDON LACE
Linens From the Past
167 Newbury Street
Boston, MA 02116
(Nottingham curtains; catalog)

MAISON ANTOINE
OLD BRUSSELS LACE SHOP
Grand' Place, 26
Brussels, Belgium
(lace and lace-accented linens, accessories)

MAZZARON
San Provolo, 4970
Fondamenta Osmarin
Venice, Italy
(lace and lace-accented linens, accessories)

paper white ltd.
P.O. Box 956
Fairfax, CA 94930
(cutwork and lace-accented bedlinens,
tablelinens, accessories, clothing; write for a
where-to-buy listing)

PEACOCK ALLEY
13720 Midway Road
Dallas, TX 75244
(cutwork and lace-accented bedlinens,
pillows, sachets; write for a where-to-buy
listing)

REMEMBRANCE OF THINGS PAST
100 North 22 Street
Philadelphia, PA 19103
(lace-accented accessories; flyer)

ROCOCO
9, Wollestraat
Bruges, Belgium
(lace and lace-accented linens, accessories)

RUE DE FRANCE
78 Thames Street
Newport, RI 02840
(French curtains, placemats, runners,
yardgoods; catalog)

SELECTION
8-14, Breidelstraat
Bruges, Belgium
(lace and lace-accented linens, accessories)

VICTORIA'S LACE DESIGNS
435 Withnell Crescent
Oakville, Ontario
Canada L6L 3MI
(lace-accented bedlinens, pillows, towels,
sachets; catalog)

WESTMINSTER LACE
1326 Fifth Avenue
Seattle, WA 98101
(lace-accented bedlinens, tablelinens, pillows,
accessories, clothing; write for a where-to-
buy listing; partial listing of shops follows:

South Coast Plaza
Costa Mesa, CA

Stanford Shopping Center
Palo Alto, CA

White Flint Mall
North Bethesda, MD

Oakbrook Center
Oak Brook, IL

WHITE LINEN, INC.
P.O. Box 88
Schodack Landing, NY 12156
(cutwork bedlinens, tablelinens; write for a
where-to-buy listing)

WOLFMAN GOLD & GOOD CO.
116 Greene Street
New York, NY 10012
(lace-accented linens, yardgoods, paper lace
trim, paper doilies)

LACEMAKING SUPPLIES

GLIMAKRA LOOMS 'N YARNS, INC.
Viking Trading Co.
and
THE UNICORN, including BOOKS FOR
CRAFTSMEN, INC.
and
VICTORIAN VIDEO PRODUCTIONS
1304 Scott Street
Petaluma, CA 94952
(lacemaking supplies, kits, books, patterns,
video tapes; catalog)

THE LACEMAKER
Lace and Needle Art
23732-G Bothell Highway S.E.
Bothell, WA 98021
(lacemaking supplies, kits, patterns, books;
catalog)

LACES & LACEMAKING
The Battenberg Specialist
and
LACE CRAFTS QUARTERLY
3201 East Lakeshore Drive
Tallahassee, FL 32312
(lacemaking supplies, kits, patterns, books,
video tapes, correspondence courses, and
ready-made collars; catalog, LCQ magazine,
by subscription)

LACIS
2982 Adeline Street
Berkeley, CA 94703
(kits, books; catalog)

LAURIKS IMPORTS
3790 El Camino Real
Palo Alto, CA 94306
(Belgian lace tapes, kits, patterns, video tapes,
and ready-made Battenberg scarves and
handkerchiefs; catalog)

MYLACE
P.O. Box 13466
Tallahassee, FL 32317
(Myline lace tapes)

ROBIN AND RUSS HANDWEAVERS
533 North Adams Street
McCinnville, OR 97128
(lacemaking supplies, books; catalog)

ROBIN'S BOBBINS
Route 1, Box 1736
Mineral Bluff, GA 30559
(lacemaking supplies, books; catalog)

SELECTED READINGS

Earnshsaw, Pat, A DICTIONARY OF LACE.
Aylesbury, Buckinghamshire, England: Shire
Publications, 1982.

————. BOBBIN & NEEDLE LACES:
Identification and Care. McMinnville, OR:
Robin and Russ Handweavers, 1983.

————. NEEDLEMADE LACES: Materials,
Designs, Techniques. London: Ward Stock
Ltd., 1988.

————. THE IDENTIFICATION OF LACE.
Aylesbury, Buckinghamshire, England: Shire
Publications, 1980

Foley, Tricia. LINENS AND LACE. New
York: Clarkson N. Potter, Inc., 1990.

Fuhrmann, Brigita. BOBBIN LACE: An
Illustrated Guide to Traditional and
Contemporary Techniques. New York: A
Dover Reprint of Watson-Guptill
Publications edition, 1976.

Hopewell, Jeffrey. PILLOW LACE AND
BOBBINS. Aylesbury, Buckinghamshire,
England: Shire Publications.

Jackson, Mrs. F. Nevill. OLD HANDMADE
LACE: With a Dictionary of Lace. New
York: A Dover Reprint. Originally published
1900.

Jourdain, Margaret. OLD LACE: A
Handbook for Collectors. London: B. T.
Batsford, reissue. Originally published 1908.

Levey, Santina M. LACE: A HISTORY.
London and Leeds, England: The Victoria &
Albert Museum, with W. S. Maney & Son,
1983.

Montupet, Janine. THE LACEMAKER. New
York: Atheneum Publishers, 1988.

———— and Ghislaine Schoeller. LACE: The
Elegant Web. New York: Harry N. Abrams,
1990.

Palliser, Mrs. Bury. THE HISTORY OF
LACE. New York: A Dover Reprint.
Originally published 1875, revised 1901.

Preston, Doris Campbell. NEEDLE-MADE
LACES AND NET EMBROIDERIES:
Reticella Work, Carrickmacross Lace,
Princess Lace, and Other Traditional
Techniques. New York: A Dover Reprint.
Originally published 1938.

Reigate, Emily. AN ILLUSTRATED GUIDE
TO LACE. Woodbridge, Suffolk, England,
Antique Collector's Club, 1986.

Wardle, Patricia. VICTORIAN LACE.
Carlton, Bedford, England: Ruth Bean, 1982.
Warwick, Kathleen and Shirley Nilsson.

LEGACY OF LACE: Identifying, Collecting,
and Preserving American Lace. New York:
Crown Publishers, 1988.

MUSEUM COLLECTIONS
United States

COOPER-HEWITT MUSEUM
The Smithsonian Institution's
National Museum of Design
2 East 91 Street
New York, NY 10128

Collections in storage; appointment must be
made through the curator to review
transparencies in the Study Center Library.
The Cooper-Hewitt advised us that there are
no lace collections open for viewing in the
United States because of concern for the
integrity of the antique laces. Consult your
local museum to ascertain if it has a
decorative arts department and a lace
collection, and if laces can be viewed for
research or study purposes.

Many European museums, especially small
museums associated with traditional lace
centers, do have collections that have never
been removed from view; a sampling follows.

Great Britain

VICTORIA AND ALBERT MUSEUM
Lace Room
Cromwell Road
London, England SW7

ROYAL SCOTTISH MUSEUM
Chambers Street
Edinburgh, Scotland EH1

THE LACE CENTER
and
MUSEUM OF COSTUME AND TEXTILES
'Severns' Building
Castle Road
Nottingham, England

Belgium

MUSEÉ DU COSTUME ET DE LA
DENTELLE
rue de la Violette, 6
Brussels

MUSÉES RAYAUX D'ART ET D'HISTOIRE
10, Parc du Cinquantenaire
Brussels

KANTCENTRUM
14, Balstratt
Bruges

France

MUSÉE DES BEAUX-ARTS ET DE LA
DENTELLE
Alençon

MUSÉE HISTORIQUE DE TISSUS
34, rue de la Charité
Lyons

MUSÉE DES ARTS DECORATIFS
rue de Rivoli, 107
Paris

Italy

JESURUM
San Marco, 4310
Ponte Canonica
Venice

SCUOLA DEI MERLETTI DI BURANO
Piazza Baldassare Galuppi
Burano, Venice

MUSEO POLDI-PEZZOLI
12, via Manzoni
Milan

LACEMAKING CLASSES

For a reference guide to lacemaking centers
and classes in the United States, Canada,
Europe, Eastern Europe, and Russia, we refer
you to the directory in LACE, The Elegant
Web, by Janine Montupet and Ghislaine
Schoeller, Harry N. Abrams, Inc., NY, 1990.

CONSERVING AND PROTECTING LACE: CONSERVATORS

AMERICAN INSTITUTE FOR
CONSERVATION OF HISTORIC AND
ARTISTIC WORKS (The AIC)
3545 Williamsburg Lane, N.W.
Washington D.C. 20008
(professional organization with listing of
conservators)

E. BRAUN
717 Madison Avenue
New York, NY 10021
(linens shop; will do restoration work)

GENTLE ARTS
Bryce Reveley, conservator
P.O. Box 15832
936 Arabella
New Orleans, LA 70115
(textile conservation)

BETTY LACASSE
37 Prescott Avenue
White Plains, NY 10605
(appraisals and textile conservation)

LACIS
2982 Adeline
Berkeley, CA 94703
(appraisals and lace restoration)

LACE LEGACY
220 South First
Kent, WA 98032
(lace restoration)

LINENS LIMITED
4411 North Oakland Avenue
Milwaukee, WI 53211
(textile conservation)

STUDIO I
6 Highland Cross
Rutherford, NJ 07070
(textile conservation)

TEXTILE CONSERVATION CENTER
Museum of American Textile History
800 Massachusetts Avenue
North Andover, MA 01845
(textile conservation, restoration)

TEXTILE CONSERVATION WORKSHOP
Patsy Orlovsky, director
Main Street
South Salem, NY 10590
(textile conservation, restoration)

HELENE VON ROSENSTIEL, INC.
382 11 Street
Brooklyn, NY 11215
(textile conservation, restoration)

CONSERVING AND PROTECTING LACE: SUPPLIES

CONSERVATION MATERIALS LTD.
240 Freeport Boulevard
Box 2884
Sparks, NE 89431
(acid-free tubes, boxes, tissue; Orvus paste
cleaning agent)

LAVANT
Sister Fisher Ltd.
575 Madison Avenue
New York, NY 10022
(cleaning agent; write for a where-to-buy
listing)

LE BLANC LINEN WASH
Active Chemicals Co., Inc.
P.O. Box 20487
St. Petersburg, FL 33742
(cleaning agent; write for a where-to-buy
listing)

PROCESS MATERIALS
30 Veterans Boulevard
Rutherfurd, NJ 07070
(acid-free tubes, boxes, tissue)

TALAS
Division of Technical Library Service, Inc.
213 West 35 Street
New York, NY 10001
(acid-free boxes, tissue; Orvus paste cleaning
agent)

LACEMAKERS' ORGANIZATIONS

INTERNATIONAL OLD LACERS, INC.
P.O. Box 16186
Phoenix, AZ 85011
(promotes interest in lacemaking, collecting,
identification, teaching, and history; directory
of members; bulletin)

THE LACE GUILD
The Hollies
53 Audmann
Stourbridge
West Midlands, England DY8
(journal)

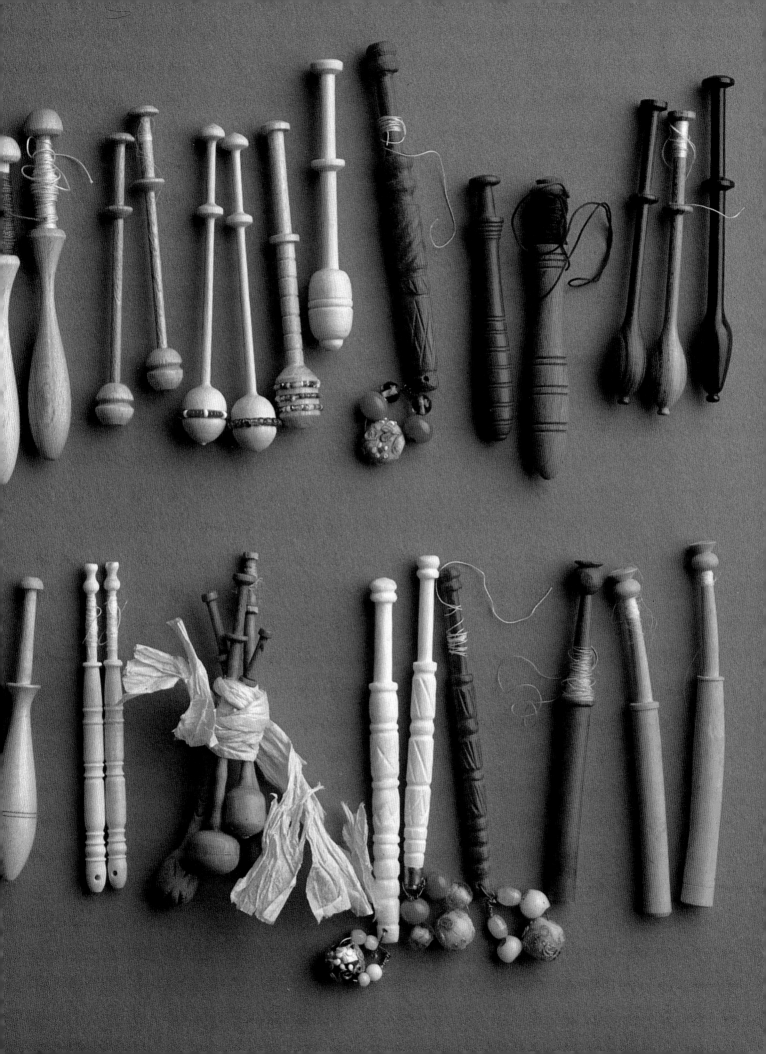

CREDITS

The following credits serve to identify various laces and accessories that were graciously loaned for the photography of specific room settings, as well as the designers of the rooms or details thereof. Addresses of shops or dealers mentioned in this listing are located in the Directory. An asterisk following a fabric manufacturer's name signifies a designer resource that is open to the trade only; the addresses given are for headquarters—you must contact them for addresses of local showrooms. At the time of this writing, laces identified by pattern name were all available. All photographs are by George Ross, except as specifically noted below; all photographs taken on location in England are by Keith Scott Morton.

Front cover: See credit for page 54.
Back cover: For photo at top, see credit for page 126; bottom left, see page 102; bottom right, see page 49 bottom.
Page 1: Bulletin board styled by Kim Freeman.
Pages 2—3: Pillowcases embellished with Alençon, princesse, and point de Venise laces and Irish crochet from Anichini Linea Casa.
Page 8: Hand-embroidered cutwork linen tablecloth covering chair from paper white ltd.
Page 9: Photograph of window by Steve Gross, Susan Daley.
Page 20: Photograph by Keith Scott Morton.
Pages 24—25: "Largo" French machine lace, used as background for all chapter openers, from jab*, available through Stroheim & Romann, Inc.*, 31-11 Thomson Avenue, Long Island City, NY 11101. Inset photograph by Keith Scott Morton.
Page 26: Detail of table, in library designed by Cullman & Kravis, Inc., 790 Madison Avenue, Suite 206, New York, NY 10021.
Pages 28—29: Room design by Charles Riley, 323 East 8 Street, New York, NY 10009. Irish crochet panel, used as curtain

next to mural, and Venetian-style lace on settee both from Trouvaille Française. Painted wall by Gail Leddy.
Pages 30—31: Room design by Bob Patino & Company, Inc., 400 East 52 Street, New York, NY 10022.
Page 32: The Astors' cottage, Beechwood, on Bellevue Avenue in Newport, Rhode Island, is open to the public during the summer months. "Fleurie" French machine lace, used in the window treatment, and "Le Jardin" tablecover, on mah-jongg table, from Rue de France.
Page 33: Pillows on sofa, fabricated from remnants of old lace, by Jule Lang.
Pages 34—35: All hand-embroidered cutwork and lace-accented linens, pillows, and accessories from paper white ltd.
Pages 36—37: Carriage house renovation by Michael Graves Architect, 341 Nassau Street, Princeton, NJ 08540.
Pages 38—39: Antique lace bertha, on wall, from Virginia Antiques. Rosebud globe accented with Nottingham lace, on table, from Fiona Barclay's Trousseau of Nottingham Lace.
Page 40: Photograph of wreath by Keith Scott Morton.
Pages 42—43: Loft designed by Vincente Wolf Associates, Inc., 333 West 39 Street, New York, NY 10018. Venetian-style needle lace on Louis XVI bench from Lace Works, Inc.
Pages 44—45: Antique tape lace flounce and runner, on mantel and chair, both from Virginia Antiques. "My Lady's Garden" Nottingham lace, over table, from Kirk-Brummel Associates, Inc.*, 826 Broadway, New York, NY 10003.
Page 48: Library setting at the Place des Antiquaires in New York City designed by McMillen, Inc., 155 East 56 Street, New York, NY 10022. Belgian lace cloth from Françoise Nunnallé. Photograph by Bill Rothschild, courtesy of McMillen, Inc.
Page 49, top: Detail of desk, styled by Charles Riley, see credit for page 28.
Page 49, bottom: "Roses Pompon" wallcovering from Brunschwig & Fils*, 75 Virginia Road, P.O. Box 905, North White Plains, NY 10603. Lace- and pearl-covered address book from Alix and Alexis.
Page 50: "Peacock on Bough" Nottingham lace panel, hanging at left, from Kirk-Brummel Associates, Inc., see credit for

page 44.
Page 51: Garden room at the Friends of Thirteen 1988 Showhouse at Chieftains designed by Barbara Ostrom Associates, Inc., One International Boulevard, Suite 209, Mahwah, NJ 07495. Lace cover, on sleigh bed, and all lace-covered pillows from Françoise Nunnallé. "Dentelle Lace," over arm of chair, from André Bon, Inc.*, 979 Third Avenue, New York, NY 10022.
Pages 52—53: Table and paintbrush painted by artist Phyllis Yes, represented by the Elizabeth Leach Gallery, 207 Southwest Pine, Portland, OR 97204.
Page 54: Detail of table, in a room setting for the Friends of Thirteen 1988 Estate Showhouse at Chieftains, designed by Robert Metzger Interiors, Inc., 215 East 58 Street, New York, NY 10022. Lace-embellished silk shawl from Françoise Nunnallé.
Page 57: Photo frames #21170 and #08995 both from the Exposures Catalog, 70 S. Main Street, South Norwalk, CT 06854.
Page 60, top: Photograph of window by Steve Gross, Susan Daley.
Page 60, bottom: "Caroline" bow-split Bavarian machine lace curtain, in window with birdcages, from Linens & Lace.
Page 61: "Geneve" diamond-cut machine lace curtain panels and valances from La Dentellière.
Pages 62—63: Hand-tinted limited-edition photograph of the Isaiah Jones Homestead Bed & Breakfast, by Norm Darwish, brochure of prints available, 298 West Chicago Road, Coldwater, MI 49036.
Pages 64—65: Photographs by Paul Kopelow.
Pages 70—71: "Peacock on Bough" Nottingham lace, used as undercover on table, from Kirk-Brummel Associates, Inc.*, see credit for page 44. Creamer, cup, and saucer from Alix and Alexis.
Page 72: Room design by Katherine Stephens, 200 East 61 Street, New York, NY 10021.
Page 73: Irish teacloth from Lucullus. Photograph by Andrew Boyd, originally published in *Verandah* magazine, used by permission.
Pages 76—77: Hand-embroidered and cutwork-accented "market" umbrella from paper white ltd.
Pages 80—81: Table settings designed by Audrey Sterling; Iron Horse sparkling wines

from Iron Horse Ranch & Vineyard, Sebastopol, CA 95472.

Page 82, top left: Tea set-up for the J. P. Stevens Company showroom in New York City designed by Stanley Hura with Beau Maas, 14 Sutton Place South, New York, NY 10022.

Pages 84–85: Dining table designed by Michael Graves Architect, see credit for page 36.

Page 86: Porch designed by Carolyn Guttila/ Plaza One, P.O. Box 670, Locust Valley, NY 11560. "Elsa" machine lace, used for curtains, from Brunschwig & Fils*, see credit for page 49, bottom. Photograph by Peter Vitale, courtesy of Brunschwig & Fils.

Page 87: Sunroom designed for the Wisteria Heights 1987 Showcase in Montclair, NJ, by Barbara Ostrom Associates, Inc., see credit for page 51.

Pages 88–89: Hand-embroidered cutwork linen cloth and napkins from paper white ltd.

Page 91: Photograph of crocheted heart by Paul Kopelow.

Page 94: Kitchen design by Motif Designs, 20 Jones Street, New Rochelle, NY 10801. "Melange de Fruits" valance from La Dentellière. Nottingham lace tablecloth from Laura Ashley.

Page 95: Room design by Cullman & Kravis, Inc., see credit for page 26.

Page 96: Fantasy room at the Place des Antiquaires in New York City designed by Noel Jeffrey, Inc. 215 East 58 Street, New York, NY 10022. Photograph by Peter Vitale, courtesy of Noel Jeffrey, Inc.

Page 97, top: Room design by Vince Mulford, Art Through Antiques, P.O. Box 45, Malden Bridge, NY 12115. Photograph by Keith Scott Morton, courtesy of *Country Living* magazine.

Page 97, bottom: Room design by Robert Currie, 109 West 27 Street, New York, NY 10001. Photograph courtesy of Robert Currie.

Page 98: Hand-embroidered cutwork linens and Cluny-style lace trim, used along ceiling beams, and "lace"-painted floorcloth from paper white ltd.

Page 99, top: Kitchen photograph by Jessie Walker, courtesy of *Country Living* magazine.

Page 99, bottom: Cupboard photograph by Kari Haavisto.

Pages 104–105: Tree seat designed and constructed by Robert Craven, Church

Cottage, Stoke Street, Milborough, Ludlow, Shropshire, England. Drinks set-up styled by Anne Hardy. Photographs by Keith Scott Morton, courtesy of *Country Living* magazine.

Pages 106–107: Paper lace shelf trim from Wolfman Gold & Good Co.

Page 108: Inset photograph by Keith Scott Morton.

Pages 110–111: Nottingham lace bedcover from Laura Ashley.

Page 112, top: Bedroom designed for the Lord & Taylor Fifth Avenue, New York, store, Winter 1988. "Roses Pompon" wallcovering from Brunschwig & Fils*, see credit for page 49, bottom.

Page 112, bottom: Photograph by Charles Nesbit, courtesy of *Country Living* magazine.

Page 113: Bedroom at the 1988 Alabama Symphony Showhouse designed by Maurine Abney Interior Design, c/o Kensington Collection, Inc., 2841 Culver Road, Mountain Brook, AL 35223. Photograph by Michael Dunne, reprinted by permission of *House Beautiful* magazine, copyright © October 1988, The Hearst Corp., all rights reserved.

Pages 116–117: Exercise room designed by Vincente Wolf Associates, Inc., see credit for page 42. "Thomasina" machine lace, swagged over curtain and draped over televisions, from Lee Jofa*, 800 Central Boulevard, Carlstadt, NJ 07072.

Page 119: "Neo-Grec" machine lace reproduction of lace panel featured at the Philadelphia Centennial Exhibition of 1876, used over shower curtain liner, from J. R. Burrows & Co.

Page 121: Bedroom at the Friends of Thirteen 1988 Showhouse at Chieftains, designed by Charles Riley, see credit for page 28.

Page 123, top: Hand-embroidered cutwork linens from paper white ltd.

Page 123, bottom: Photograph of cradle by Paul Kopelow.

Page 124, top: For stores carrying the Ralph Lauren Home Collection, including bedlinens, write 1185 Avenue of the Americas, New York, NY 10036. The collection is available at the Polo Ralph Lauren Shop, 867 Madison Avenue, New York, NY 10021, and Polo Ralph Lauren shops in Brussels, Munich, Toronto, Montreal, Hong Kong, and throughout Japan. Photograph by François Halard, courtesy of the Ralph Lauren Home Collection.

Page 124, bottom: "Grand-Mere" machine-loomed crochet window treatments and "Laurier" comforter from Rue de France.

Page 125: Linen apron from paper white ltd.

Pages 126–127: Room design by Lyn Henderson Fabacher, Henderson Interiors, 1535 Webster Street, New Orleans, LA 70118, in collaboration with Bremermann Designs, 301 Chartres Street, New Orleans, LA 70130.

Page 129, bottom: Atomizer, potpourri ball, and powder bottles from Alix and Alexis.

Pages 130–131: Room setting at the J. P. Stevens Company showroom in New York City designed by Stanley Hura, see credit for page 82, top left.

Pages 134–135: Mignon Faget jewelry available at Mignon Faget, 710 Dublin Street, New Orleans, LA 70118. Normandy lace bedspread from Lace Works, Inc.

Page 136: Photograph by Antoine Bootz, courtesy of Noel Jeffrey, Inc., see credit for page 96.

Page 137: Photograph by Kari Haavisto.

Pages 140–141: "Old Calais" bed canopy, duvet cover, and curtains, and "Alouette" pillow shams from Rue de France.

Pages 142–143: All nursery accessories from Linda Evans Remembers. Hand-tinted limited-edition photograph by Norm Darwish, see credit for page 62.

Page 144: Bedroom at the Friends of Thirteen 1988 Showhouse at Chieftains designed by Feldman • Hagan Interiors, 135 East 74 Street, New York, NY 10021. "Albi" machine lace, at window, from André Bon, Inc.*, see credit for page 51. American-made bedcover from Ruth Arzt.

Pages 146–147: Photographs by Cookie Kinkead.

Pages 148–149: Photograph by Bo Niles.

Page 150: Photograph of Catherine Buckley's shop in London by Keith Scott Morton.

Pages 152–159: Textile conservation procedures photographed at Bryce Reveley's Gentle Arts Studio in New Orleans, LA.

Page 161: Photograph by Keith Scott Morton.

Page 162: Rolls of French machine lace photographed at the Rue de France shop in Newport, RI.

Pages 168–169: Antique bobbins from the collection of Alexander Heinritz.

Page 172: Lace pillow, see credit above.

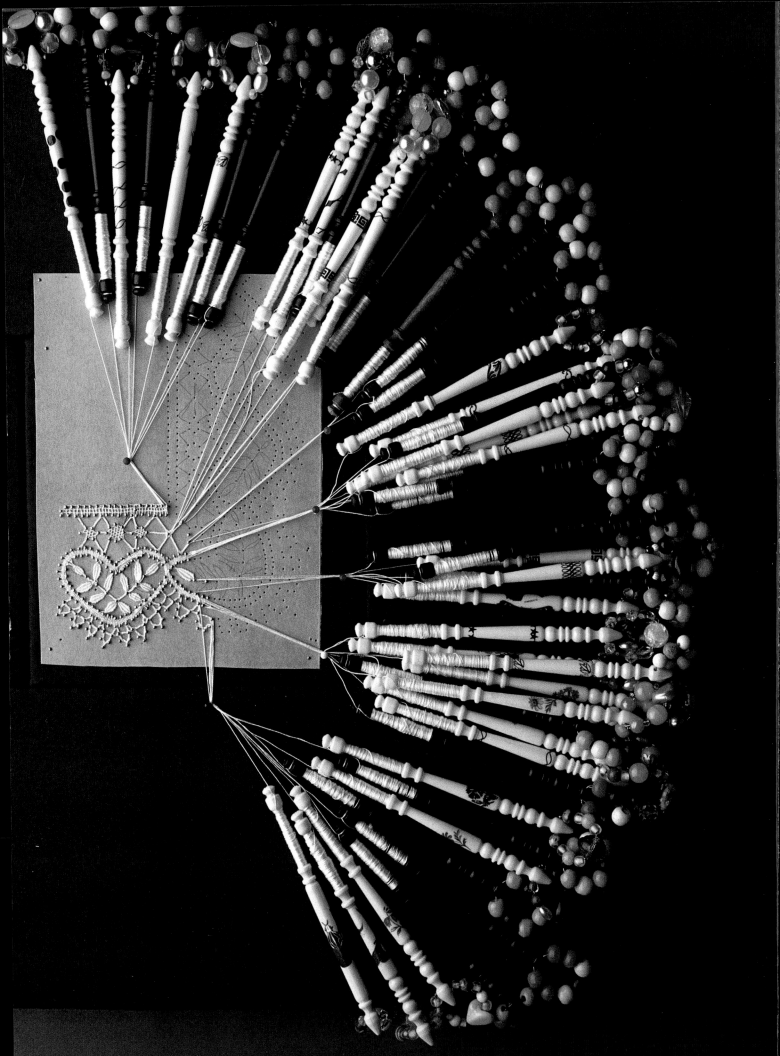

ACKNOWLEDGMENTS

It is no small task to write a book; many are to be thanked for their help and cooperation in the production of this one:

To friends who welcomed me and offered hospitality, and a bed, during photography shoots on location: In New Orleans, Bethany and Johann Bultman, who also provided entree to all the locations we photographed in that city; in London, Anne and Jim Hardy (I am especially grateful to Anne for transporting us to our locations outside of the city, and to following up via international fax and phone lines on our behalf); in Newport, Rhode Island, Mary Shepard, and also Pam Kelley of Rue de France; and in San Francisco, Julie and Fred Altshuler, and also Jan Dutton of paper white ltd.

To friends old and new connected by the thread of lace, and to family, designers, and lace collectors who opened their houses to photography for the book—and especially to my mother, Ann Thorne, who allowed me to create a half-dozen lacy vignettes in my parents' apartment.

To all the manufacturers and shops—mentioned in the Credits or in the Directory—who loaned or donated laces for use in photographs, and especially to Richard Kirkham and Rod Pleasants of Kirk-Brummel, to Elke Kasman on behalf of Brunschwig & Fils and André Bon, and to Larry Bilotti at Laura Ashley whose donated machine-loomed lace yardage proved invaluable for photo propping on several occasions.

To Margaret Caselton, formerly of British *Country Living,* and now home editor of *Options* in London, who led me to Virginia Wetherell and to Catherine Buckley's shop, and to Keith Scott Morton, for his photography of these London locations as well as the orangerie and nursery kitchen in the West Country.

To the photographers, credited on the preceding pages, who graciously complemented my coverage with wonderful shots from their personal archives, so that I could supplement locations, and to Rachel Newman, editor at *Country Living,* who released several previously published photographs from the magazine for use herein.

To George Ross, who, as principal photographer, applied his vision and expertise to this delicate subject with great finesse and precision, and to his wife, Sally, whose graceful styling is displayed in several of the locations.

To Roy Finamore, who guided the book almost to its completion, and free-lance editor Gretchen Salisbury, who took the book in hand in its final stages.

To Andy Stewart, Leslie Stoker, Mary Albi, José Pouso, and the entire staff at Stewart, Tabori & Chang who believe that a book must be as beautiful as possible, and

To Julio Vega, whose elegant design ensured that this book would be.

To Veronica McNiff, whose gift of the Dover edition of Mrs. Bury Palliser's "History of Lace" launched my own library on the subject and whose introduction to the curators at the Cooper-Hewitt museum led me to the Lace Guild of New York where I tried my hand at making bobbin lace.

To Bryce Reveley, whose welcome into her conservation studio and home reinforced my respect for antique linens and laces and their care, and to Pat Earnshaw, whose cautionary letter on preserving antique lace was well appreciated.

To Jo Bidner, whose counsel and encouragement proved invaluable during my readings and all-too-cursory study of lace.

And to my family—Bill, David, and Peter —who put up with my travel binges and long weekend sieges at the word processor to make the writing deadline.

INDEX

Alençon lace, 19, 20
American Institute of Conservation, 152
antimacassars, 21, 103, 120
antique lace, 23, 28, 57, 91, 95, 111, 134, 140
    caring for, 23, 152–160
    directory of sources for, 163–164
    stains on, 157

bars (stitches), 15
bathrooms, 109, 119, 124, 139, 146
Battenberg lace, 23, 27, 103
bed curtains, 113, 114, 130
bedlinens, 109, 113, 114, 123, 134, 144, 145
    blocking of, 156, 157
    storing of, 160
    wet-cleaning of, 152–156
bedrooms, 108–149
Belgium, 13, 18, 20, 21, 49
bertha, 37
blocking lace, 156, 157, 158
bobbin (pillow) lace, 10, 13, 17
borders, 11, 54, 82
brides (stitches), 15
broderie anglaise, 89
Bruges, 21
Bruges lace, 98
Brussels lace, 20, 145
bureau scarf, 120
buttonhole stitches, 12–13

candle wax stains, 157, 158
canopy, 114, 140
caring for lace:
    antique, 23, 152–160
    new machine-made, 152
Carrickmacross, 23
Chantilly lace, 19, 72, 81
christening dresses, 35
cleaning lace, 152–158
    products for, 153
    removing stains from, 157–158
    wet-cleaning method of, 152–156, 158
Cluny-style lace, 32, 98
collars, 17, 28, 37, 54
conservators, 152, 157
    directory of, 167
conserving lace, supplies for, 167

convents, lacemaking schools
    affiliated with, 14
Costume Society of America, 152
cotton, 20–21, 23, 152, 153, 159
creases, 158
crochet, 21, 25, 91, 114, 124
    dimestore, 45, 91
    Irish, 23, 28, 120
crocheted tablecloths, 63, 81, 97
cupboard and shelf trimmings, 57, 69, 78, 82,
    98, 99, 105
curtains, 32, 57, 72, 78, 87, 109, 119, 124,
    136, 139
    blocking of, 156, 157
    ironing of, 158, 159
    storing of, 160
    valance, 60, 69, 94, 98, 124, 139
    wet-cleaning of, 152–156
cutwork, 23, 25, 27
    apron, 124
    curtains, 139
    tablecloths, 69, 89, 97

dimestore lace, 57, 69, 130
    crochet, 45, 91
dining rooms, 68–107
directory, 163–167
discoloration, 160
dogs, in lace smuggling, 18
doilies, 21, 69, 78, 82, 103
    storing of, 159–160
dotted swiss, 27
dry cleaning lace, 152
drying lace, 156–157, 158
duchesse lace, 49

Earnshaw, Pat, 11, 12
Edict of Nantes, 18–19
Edward III, King of England, 17
Elizabeth I, Queen of England, 18
emigration, 19
England, 10, 17, 19, 21
eyelet, 23

falling collar, 17
fan, 103, 129
filet, 23, 74, 91, 113, 129, 139
filet tirata, 54
"finger" border, 120
Flanders lace, 18
flax, 13–14
"flycovers," 100
French lace, 10, 19, 20, 21, 32, 57, 91, 114

Gentle Arts studio, 152, 155
grease stains, 157, 158

handkerchief linens, 109
handkerchiefs, 65, 103, 128
    blocking of, 156, 157
    storing of, 159–160
handmade lace:
    bobbin, 10, 13, 17
    history of, 10–20, 21–23
    needle, see needle lace
hand-washing lace, 152–158
Henry III, King of France, 17
Henry IV, King of France, 17
Honiton lace, 21
hydrogen peroxide, 153, 155

Industrial Revolution, 19–20, 151
insertions, 65
insets, 11
Irish crochet, 23, 28, 120
ironing lace, 158–159

Jacquard, Joseph-Marie Charles, 20
Josephine, Empress of France, 19

knots, picot, 15, 40
lace:
    "breathing" required by, 23, 160
    caring for, 23, 152–160
    defined, 11
    derivation of word, 10
    development of design techniques in, 11–12
    handling and storage of, 152, 159–160
    history of, 10–23
    making of, see lacemaking
    popularity of, 10, 12, 14, 16, 17
    use of, 23
    see also handmade lace; machine-made lace
"Lace Lady, The," 10
lacemakers' organizations, 167
lacemaking, 21, 69
    classes in, 167
    history of, 14–16
    supplies for, 166
lacemaking machines (looms), 13, 19–20, 25
lace papers, 57, 69, 99, 105
lace-washers, professional, 151
"lacis", 10
layette, 140
Leavers, John, 19
Le Puy, 21
Levers machine, 19–20
lightening lace, 155
Limerick lace, 23
linen, 11, 13–14, 15, 21, 74, 109, 152, 153,
    159
linens, 89, 109, 114, 152
    caring for, 23, 152